CHRISTIANITY AND ECONOMICS

IS VOLUME

90

OF THE

Twentieth Century Encyclopedia of Catholicism

UNDER SECTION

IX

THE CHURCH AND THE MODERN WORLD

IT IS ALSO THE

58TH

VOLUME IN ORDER OF PUBLICATION

Edited by **HENRI DANIEL-ROPS** *of the Académie Française*

CHRISTIANITY AND ECONOMICS

By CHRISTOPHER HOLLIS

HAWTHORN BOOKS · PUBLISHERS · *New York*

First Edition, January, 1961

NIHIL OBSTAT

Joannes M. T. Barton, S.T.D., L.S.S.

Censor Deputatus

IMPRIMATUR

E. Morrogh Bernard

Vicarius Generalis

Westmonasterii, die XXIX OCTOBRIS MCMLX

CONTENTS
1135935

I. THE CHURCH AND ECONOMICS   7
  Economics and the Gospel   7
  Economics and the Early Church   13
  The Medieval Church   18
  Post-Reformation Developments   24

II. THE CHURCH AND NINETEENTH-CENTURY
  ECONOMICS   29
  Before *Rerum Novarum*   29
  Leo XIII and *Rerum Novarum*   35
  Catholics and *Rerum Novarum*   43

III. PIUS XI   50
  Quadragesimo Anno   51
  The Corporative State   54
  Germany and Italy   58
  The Changed Economic Situation since Leo
    XIII's Time   59
  A Monetary Crisis   63
  The Church and Socialism   66
  Catholic Political Parties   73

IV. THE CHURCH AND INTERNATIONAL SOCIAL JUSTICE   77

V. CATHOLICISM AND THE POPULATION QUESTION   95
  The Shifting Balance of Population   95
  Birth Control   96
  Increase of Population Matched by Increased
    Food Production   98
  Fallacious Arguments for Restriction of Popu-
    lation   102
  Immigration and Emigration   107

  SELECT BIBLIOGRAPHY   111

CHAPTER I

THE CHURCH AND
ECONOMICS

It is not the business of this book to state the apologetic case
either for the Christian revelation or for the Catholic Church,
nor to defend nor to condemn any particular economic programme. Its business is to describe the teaching of the Catholic
Church on economics—the effect which the Catholic Church
has had and ought to have had on the development of the
world's economy.

ECONOMICS AND THE GOSPEL

It is the claim of the Catholic Church that she is the Body
founded by Almighty God. Our first task must then be to ask
what teaching on economics is to be found in the New
Testament or in the recorded words of our Lord. For all the
claims that have sometimes been made for Christ as the first
Socialist, there is in fact nothing in the Gospels to suggest
that he was at all interested in setting out an economic system.
The only direct teaching on economics to be found in the
Gospels is St John the Baptist's advice to Roman soldiers to
be content with their wages, and it is reasonable to think that
St John gave that advice not because he had studied the
details of the Roman pay system and reached the conclusion
that the Imperial Treasury was paying out exactly the just
wage, but because in general he thought it foolish that posses-
sors of immortal souls should surrender to discontent over a
matter of such secondary importance as their standard of

living. So Christ's concern was to call sinners to repentance, to offer to those that heard him an everlasting life of companionship with God beyond the grave.

To the preacher of such a Gospel the material standards of this life, where moth and rust doth corrupt, were, as to John, of secondary importance.   But, unlike John, our Lord was no extreme ascetic. He was quite content to take social life as he found it—to eat with publicans if he was invited—to allow precious ointment to be wasted in a burst of generosity rather than carefully sold and the proceeds given to the poor—and, if as a result of such social life, he was called "a gluttonous man and a wine-bibber" he was indifferent. A high standard of living was in itself neither good nor bad. It was dangerous because fallen man tended to set his heart where his treasure lay—to love riches when he possessed them—and he who loved riches condemned himself to unhappiness because he had set his love on that which could not endure. Therefore our Lord advised a particular rich young man to sell all that he had and give to the poor, warned the rich that it was easier for the camel to go through the eye of a needle than for them to be saved, and in general spoke as if it was a great ill fortune to be rich and a great good fortune to be poor. He did not demand that the rich should give to the poor in order to make the poor in their turn rich. If riches were a danger, they would be just as dangerous to those who were now poor, should they acquire them, as they are today to those who are now rich. The modern politician speaks of doubling the standard of living and his hearers all too often take it for granted that his promises are desirable. All that to them is in question is whether they can be performed. But there is nothing in the New Testament to suggest that Christ would have thought such an ambition desirable. At the best it would have seemed to him irrelevant to the main purpose of life—in practice almost certainly a stumbling block to that main purpose— since such a raising of standards could only be achieved by a concentration of attention to an inordinate degree on material things.

We used to tell one another that poverty was the cause of crime. Today in almost every white country of the world we have a material standard where people "have never had it so good" and a disturbing increase in crime for which sociologists are puzzled to know the reason. Nor did our Lord ever say anything which indicated an interest in so rearranging the affairs of society as to increase its total production.

It is true that we are told in the Acts of the Apostles of an apparent experiment in primitive communism among the early disciples. There is no claim that in making this experiment they were acting on any explicit instruction of our Lord's. In the Gospels Zacchaeus, who had given half his goods to the poor, was not commanded to give the other half. Nevertheless it is reasonable to assume that they were behaving in a way of which they at least thought that he would have approved. Yet it is important to note that this experiment, whatever exactly it implied, did not apparently imply the total abolition of private property among Christians. There was some sort of voluntary pooling of income among them for the common good, but Ananias and Sapphira are specifically told by St Peter that, even as Christians, they would have been totally free to keep for themselves some, or all, of their property, had they wished. Their sin was not that they had not surrendered all their property but that they had lied about it—pretending that they had surrendered all when they had not done so. In any event the experiment does not seem to have been a success. There was famine among the Christians in Jerusalem. Whether they shared their goods in common because there was a famine or whether there was a famine because they shared their goods in common is not quite apparent. At least, if we may assume from what happened in Jerusalem that such an experiment did not appear to the early disciples to be in any way contrary to Christ's teaching, we may equally assume from the fact that the experiment was never apparently repeated anywhere else that our Lord had never explicitly demanded such conduct as obligatory. For the Christian it is of obligation so to organize society that the necessities of everyone

are satisfied. Whether that end is best achieved by the preservation or by the abolition of private property is a question
of judgement dependent on circumstances.

Our Lord enjoined obedience to the Jewish law, and the
Jewish law explicitly recognized a right of property, and a
number of the parables—the parable of the talents, the parable
of the eleventh hour, the parable of the unjust steward—themselves clearly imply a system of property rights. If we were to
consider them simply as economic tracts, we might deduce
from the parable of the talents that our Lord believed in a
right of capitalist accumulation or from the other two parables
that the owner of property had an almost irresponsible right
to do what he liked with his own. It would obviously be
absurd to interpret them so narrowly. The lessons that they
carry are general religious and moral lessons rather than
lessons merely of economic doctrine. Our Lord drew his
illustrations from economic examples simply because such
examples came conveniently to hand. All that we can fairly
deduce from them is that he did not feel ownership to be
intrinsically wicked.

The commands not to steal and not to covet a neighbour's
goods imply a right of ownership, and, it might be argued,
if there is a right of ownership, then there must be a defining
authority and a defining doctrine to settle in doubtful cases
what belongs to A and what to B. It seems to be our Lord's
advice to his disciples to sidestep that second problem in all
doubtful cases by conceding the point at issue. If there is
dispute, avoid it by conceding the other man's claim, whether
he has strict right on his side or not. If he bids you go with
him one mile, go two. If he asks for your coat, give him also
your cloak. There is more important business in life than
arguing about coats and distances. The masters of the Jewish
Law answered at the time, and the casuists of a later day were
substantially to answer, that the result of such easy casualness
—of the literal refusal to take any thought for tomorrow—
would reduce society to chaos. The casuists couched their
answer for obvious reasons in the polite phraseology of a

distinction between counsels of perfection and the precepts of everyday life, but their answer was essentially the same as that of the masters of the Jewish Law. Those who have refused to demand of every person in a normal society full, literal obedience to the counsels of perfection—whether of turning the other cheek, of taking no thought for the morrow or the other counsels—have sometimes been accused of attempting a dishonest and impossible compromise between God and Mammon. The point is not valid. It is probable that the early disciples lived in an expectation of the imminent end of the world. If the world was going to come to an end in a year or two's time, many economic maxims, obedience to which are essential for the life of a continuing society, become obviously irrelevant. But, quite apart from that, our Lord never appeared to envisage any society in which the Christians would be sufficiently powerful in any way to influence legislation. It is always assumed that they will be a small, and probably persecuted, minority—"a light shining in the darkness"—"a voice crying in the wilderness". And, if they are also to be the lump that leaveneth the whole lump, there is no suggestion that they should exercise that influence by political, still less, by military action. It is to be exercised by spiritual means and by the force of example. So, though the problem of the attitude of the Christian towards the civil power is considered and he is bidden as a general rule to accept it— to render to Caesar, by our Lord—to honour the king, by St Peter[1]—yet there is no suggestion that the Christian will have any say in what the policy of Caesar or the king will be, whether on economic or on other matters. The pagan will promulgate the law. The Christian—except where it is in contradiction with the higher law revealed to him—will obey it.

Yet, if it is the general teaching of the Christian religion that economics, since they are concerned with the things of this world, are only of secondary importance, it does not follow from that that they are of no importance. According

[1] 1 Peter 2. 13.

to an oriental religion, such as Buddhism, this world is wholly evil, its goods an illusion. The religious man should show to it no attitude except contempt. Such is not the Christian attitude. Christianity is not only the religion of God but the religion of God made Man. In our moments of deepest disillusion and most bitter weariness with our fellow human beings we must remember that "these are they for whom their Omnipotent Creator did not disdain to die" and that "God so loved the world that he gave his only-begotten Son". This world is not the ultimate reality. But at the same time it is not mere offal. God created the world and saw that it was good. It is the testing place. As well as our duty towards God, we have a duty towards our neighbour—derived perhaps in the last analysis from the fact that our neighbour was made in the image of God, but nevertheless in itself real and urgent. "The Church," said Pius XII in his Allocution to the Consistory of February 20th, 1946, "cannot lock herself away, inert in the secrecy of her temples, and thus desert the mission that the divine Providence has entrusted to her, to form the complete man and cooperate unceasingly thereby in establishing the solid foundation of society." Therefore the Catholic Church is necessarily interested in man's economic activities as she is interested in all his activities. But it is important to understand what is the nature of her interest. People ask what is the teaching of the Church on economic or political problems. Some welcome what they call "the Catholic solution." Others see an easy and absolute dichotomy between politics and religion and say that the Church has no business to interfere in politics. Both those who call for "Catholic answers" and those who object to them have a very imperfect understanding of the nature of the problem. The Church is the vehicle of the teaching of Christ. She can only impose as dogmas teaching which was implicit in the deposit of faith which Christ left, and, as we have seen, such teaching did not include economic theories as such. Therefore it is only to a very limited extent that the Church supplies answers to economic problems. Popes issue their encyclicals, but these encyclicals, important and deserving of respect as they are, do not claim dogmatic authority nor do they pretend to give concrete answers which will tell the faithful what exact measures, or what political party, to support. They are concerned with an enunciation of principles derived both from revelation and from the natural law, which is accessible to the unaided reason—"the unchangeable principles", as Pius XI put it in *Quadragesimo Anno*, "drawn from right reason and divine revelations". They not only leave the faithful the right but they impose on them the duty of deciding for themselves which policy in an actual world they should on the balance of the arguments support. In the economic field it is only to a very limited extent that the Church tells the faithful what are the answers that they should give. Her main concern is to tell them the questions that they should ask. The Church insists that a Christian should apply to all economic problems, as he must apply to all secular problems of all sorts, the principle of the common good. The Church does not tell us whether it is for the common good that—shall we say?—the mines should be nationalized. The answer to that question depends upon all sorts of technical considerations upon which Catholics, like everybody else, both do and ought to differ from one another. But the Church would rebuke the royalty owner who should take his stand against nationalization in indifference to the general good but simply because he wanted to keep his royalties, or the miner, who would support nationalization in indifference to the general good and simply because he thought that nationalization would benefit the miners.

ECONOMICS AND THE EARLY CHURCH

It would be beyond our task to attempt to trace in detail the story of the decline of the imperial power in Western Europe in the first three centuries of the Christian era. It is sufficient to insist on the two relevant points: that the period was full of civil strife and disputed successions and that eventually with Constantine the Emperor himself decided, from whatever mixture of motives, that the civil authority would be strengthened if the Emperor should call himself Christian. That in the closing years of the Western Empire the Emperors were usually Christians, though by no means necessarily Catholic—many of them were Arians—is of importance, but it does not necessarily follow that the Church has to take responsibility for all of their policies, economic or otherwise. But it did inevitably mean that the ecclesiastical authorities had to give their minds to a problem which in the first century of Christianity they had hardly had to consider at all—the problem of what type of economic arrangements the Church would like to see. The anarchy of the times, the absence over long periods and large areas in the Western world, of any effective secular authority or of intellectual laymen, compelled both the pope and the local bishops to take to themselves secular powers which, had there been an effective State, would naturally have been left to that State. They had therefore to evolve a corpus of economic theory by means of which to judge, whether for approval or for disapproval, the actions of the State. In times of disputed authority people inevitably turned to the Church to ask which was the authority which they should obey. St Augustine, writing in the time of barbarian invasions and of the sack of Rome, laid down the principle that authority could only be authority in so far as it came from God and that empires not based on justice were no more than "great robberies". Such a principle inevitably imposed on the Church the duty of deciding what justice was. It was for her a new duty. Our Lord had indeed told Pontius Pilate that he could have had no authority had it not been given him by God, but our Lord did not take it upon himself to judge Pilate or his policies, other than by implication, or to decide between him and a rival for the procuratorship of Judaea. Circumstances imposed upon the Church a task, for which she had not asked, of judging secular rulers and secular policies.

Had the central secular power regained its vigour, the Church might possibly have accepted her new rôle as simply a rôle of emergency and withdrawn, when the emergency passed, to an exclusive concern with purely spiritual matters. Things did not turn out like that. On the contrary, for more than a thousand years Christendom was to be a city under siege—first from the barbarians, afterwards from the Mohammedans. There were times during the long years of battle when its survival appeared hardly probable. It emerged from them at the last, alive indeed but gravely wounded. In the early years of Christianity Christianity's most vigorous provinces had been those of Asia and Africa. It was in itself an Asian religion. The intellectual contribution of Europe to Christian thought had been negligible in Christianity's early centuries. Christianity's two principal provinces in Asia and Africa were entirely destroyed by the Mohammedan attack. In Europe, the Turks destroyed the Eastern Empire and made themselves masters of the Balkan Peninsula. There was a long time during which it looked as if the Moorish Sultans would succeed in establishing themselves finally in Spain.

This experience of a thousand years of siege had a profound effect on Christianity's development in economic as in other affairs. The very name and conception of Christendom—a dominion or temporal power of Christians—would have seemed very strange to the early disciples, who had been taught so plainly by our Lord that his Kingdom was not of this world. Before a threat of destruction it was forced on the later Christians by circumstances rather than adopted by choice. Under the influence of our Lord's saying about turning the other cheek and St Paul's command not to resist evil, the early Christians, even those of them who were not as Jews forbidden military service, tended towards pacifist views. Military service was not, it is true, specifically forbidden to a Christian. The centurion was not commanded to resign his commission any more than Zacchaeus had been commanded to resign his wealth. But the whole story of the Passion, of our Lord's rebuke to Peter for cutting off Malchus' ear, of his refusal of the twelve legions of angels, tended to lead the Christian to believe that the only true victories were spiritual victories and that a victory won by force was not a real victory.

In the same way Christianity came into a world whose economic system was based on slavery. It is true that there was no slavery among the Palestinian Jews and that therefore slave-owning and slavery are not apparent in the actual Gospel story. Nevertheless, as soon as Christianity spread among the Gentiles and beyond the confines of Palestine, it came into contact with slavery. What was its attitude? There is no specific condemnation of slavery in the recorded sayings of our Lord nor anywhere else in the New Testament. St Paul in his Epistle to Philemon asks Philemon to take back his runaway slave, Onesimus. He asks him in view of Onesimus' services to Paul not to think of him any longer as a slave. There is no suggestion of a general condemnation of the institution of slavery—rather a specific assertion that Onesimus had done wrong in running away from his master. The bond of a common faith which unites Jew and Gentile, man and woman, free man and slave in the unity of Jesus Christ, was of course to Paul of enormously greater importance than any difference of economic status. But the difference of economic status is not in itself specifically condemned. The teaching of the Gospels is not one of outright condemnation of any social institution but rather that social and economic institutions are of secondary importance and the slave is therefore advised to accept his lot rather than dissipate his energies in futile rebellion. There is insistence rather on the concrete act of charity—on the duty of those with money to spare to give to those who lacked it—than on criticism of a system. There is plenty of evidence that from the beginnings of Christianity— from Apostolic times—Christians accepted this obligation. The Acts tells us of Christians' work of charity in Jerusalem and the Epistles to the Romans and the Corinthians of that in Macedonia and Achaia. When the typhus broke out in Alexandria in A.D. 268 the Christian priests accepted the obligation to relieve the necessities not only of the Christian but also of the pagan poor. Julian the Apostate, planning his counter-attack against Christianity, wrote, "Is it not a shame that the impious Galileans support not only their own poor but also ours, while we neglect altogether to make provision for them?"[2]

Nevertheless the growth of Christianity undoubtedly threatened the institution of slavery not so much because it made people unwilling to be slaves as because, as we learn from the first Epistle of Clement and again from Ignatius of Antioch's Letter to Polycarp,[3] it made them unwilling to be slave-owners. The Christian faith did not denounce other relations between men than those of religion, but it inevitably caused those other relations to appear of secondary importance. Two Christians, herded together in persecution in the catacombs, the one a slave and the other a slave-owner, could not but feel that the religion which they had in common was of far more importance than the social and economic difference which divided them, and it was but natural, it required no explicit command of the Church, that the slave-owner, mindful of the command to do unto others what he would they should do unto him, should abolish that difference by manumission—that slavery among Christians should die out from its intrinsic incompatibility with Christian teaching. In 321 the code of the Emperor Theodosius recognized enfranchisement of slaves as legally binding if registered before a Catholic bishop.[4]

Yet the Christian attitude towards military service and slavery alike was inevitably modified by the Empire's official adoption of Christianity. The common objection to the pacifist is of course, "If everybody behaved like you, what would be the result?" To the early Christian such a question was meaningless for two reasons. First, he thought of the Christians as a small, uninfluential, persecuted minority. There was no need to bother about the consequence if too many people behaved like Christians. The trouble was that all too few behaved like them. Secondly, the Empire, at any rate under certain Emperors—under a Nero or a Domitian—behaved so atrociously towards Christians that many early Christians—

---

2 Sozomen, *Historia Ecclesiastica*, 4. 16.
3 I Clement, 55; Ignatius, *Ad Polycarpum*, 4.
4 *Codex Theodosii*, 4. 7. 1.

as, for instance, the author of the Apocalypse—would have thought it a good rather than an evil had the Empire collapsed.

THE MEDIEVAL CHURCH

St John Chrysostom and St Ambrose had both preached doctrines that came near to a denial of a right to property. "It is because a few men attempt to appropriate to themselves what belongs to all that disputes and wars break out," wrote Chrysostom, "as if nature were outraged that man with his chilly Yours and Mine should import division into the unity ordained by God."[5] He also wrote: "These words Yours and Mine have no meaning whatever."[6] "The Lord God ordained that this earth should be the common possession of all men," wrote St Ambrose, "and that its fruits should be enjoyed by all; it is greed that has engendered the rights of property."[7] But having no responsibility for the organization of society, these early saints, insisting on the right of all men to a share in the consumption of the world's goods, had not considered the question, so present to the mind of St Thomas Aquinas, how without property the productive life of society could be organized. With a Christian Empire there was a new situation. The Christian body took upon itself a quasi-military pattern which would have seemed very strange to the early Christian. Military qualities which had previously been held in contempt came to be held in honour. The soldier-saint made his appearance. With the weakening and eventual collapse of the central authority in the Western world, with the constant barbarian threat, self-defence compelled the estate or manor to become the real unit of organization, and under the feudal system that unit became both the military and the economic unit.

As Christians so grew in power and number as to be able to have an influence over policy and eventually indeed even to become masters of the Empire, ecclesiastical authorities found themselves faced with problems on which the teaching of the

[5] In 1 Tim., Hom. 12.
[6] In 1 Cor., Hom. 10, 3.
[7] In Psalm 118, 8. 22.

Gospel gave no direct guidance. Pope Gregory VII entrusted to Gratian, whose Decretum was completed before 1142, and a number of other theologians, the task of drawing up the "pronouncements" of the social teaching of the Church in this new society. The new teachers had to answer two questions which it was important to keep separate. On the one hand, they had to decide what was the ideal Christian solution of the problems, economic and otherwise, and to use what influence they could to ensure that Christian rulers adopted such solutions. On the other hand, they had also to decide the quite different question what policies were so flagrantly anti-Christian that they must be denounced as sins, that those who followed them must be barred from the sacraments, that confessors must be forbidden to give them absolution unless they showed penitence and purpose of amendment. There was a large intermediate gap between the perfect and the intolerable. Now the feudal system was obviously brought into existence by the pressure of secular circumstances. It was an arrangement adopted because in dangerous times it seemed to offer the best hope of survival. In so far as it implied a concentration of property and power into fewer hands, it was a system which was to some extent repugnant to Christian principles, with their insistence on the corrupting force of power and riches. The Church accepted it not because it was desirable but because it was necessary—at least not so patently undesirable and unnecessary as to deserve ecclesiastical condemnation. No one could pretend that it was a system especially commended by Christ nor that there was any reason why it should not be modified in the future as circumstances changed. It was only a Catholic system in so far as it was a system that was in fact used by Catholics. All that the Church had to say about it was that there was nothing intrinsically immoral in it—that, as has been said, it need not be condemned.

The distinction is vital. The Church teaches, of course, a contempt for riches, and by this very teaching makes in spite of herself, in so far as she is obeyed, an important economic contribution. The proportion of his income which a man above the subsistence level spends on the necessities of life is small. Even the proportion which he spends on those social entertainments which are necessary to make him an agreeable member of society, or on those things which really give him pleasure for their own sake, is small. By far the greater part is spent on vanity, on appearances, on what the modern phrase calls "keeping up with the Joneses" or what Veblen called "conspicuous waste". The sensible Christian will not spend much on such folly—not because he is explicitly forbidden to do so by the Church but because it will appear to him to be folly. He will not allow himself to measure his success in life by his income. He will observe that, though perhaps he himself is always looking to see what sort of figure he cuts with his neighbour, his neighbour does not notice him much and does not care much about him when he does notice him. He will say with Thomas à Kempis, "Be not angry that you cannot make others as you wish them to be, since you cannot make yourself as you wish to be". Therefore a Christian population will spend less on silly luxuries—not so much because the luxuries are forbidden as because they are boring—and this fact must of itself have a considerable economic effect. In so far as the advertiser is concerned merely to inform the public what goods are available and informs it in a reasonably attractive manner, his is a legitimate activity, but obviously the modern advertiser cannot pretend that such an ambition accounts for more than a modicum of his activities. In so far as he is concerned with persuading people to buy goods that he knows that they do not really want or which he does not care whether they really want them or not, his activities are not Christian activities. Similarly, a Christian, endowed with a sense of vocation, will necessarily not only live frugally but will also work hard.

Suarez is very right in refuting the Calvinist theory that "dominion is founded on grace", but it is an inevitable truth that grace does to some extent lead to dominion. It would be hard to argue, whether in the financial, the industrial or the political world, that the qualities of virtue were generally the qualities which led to supreme success, but in the middle way of life honesty is by and large the best policy. John Wesley by no means held that riches were the reward of virtue, but he warned his followers that on the contrary, if they were virtuous, they were all too likely to be prosperous and that prosperity was very dangerous to the soul. It is of course for that reason among others that the Church has always been so insistent that he who finds himself with a superfluity should give it away, or at least see that it is used for the general good.

It is not therefore necessary in such a work as this to describe the detailed organization of medieval European society. All that is necessary is to understand the basic philosophical conceptions of the medieval mind. The medieval thinkers felt the necessity of reconciling the Christian doctrine of the equality of man with the apparently obvious fact that subordination, authority and coercion were necessary for society's survival. This they did by saying that by nature man was free and equal and there was no such thing as private property but that authority and property had become necessary because of man's sinfulness after the Fall. Private property did not exist "by nature". It existed only "by convention". And, that being so, the rights of property were very different from the absolute rights, proclaimed in a later age. They were dependent on their proper use. "A man who does not use his property rightly," says St Augustine, "has no real claim on it." "A man has only a right," says St Thomas Aquinas, "to those things which he needs. Any superfluity he has a duty, not in charity but in justice, to give to others."[8] He said also: "The right of private property is not opposed to natural law but is an addition to it, devised by human reason."[9] The private right of property is subordinate to the general right of usage. The medieval economy was not for the most part a money economy. On the manor payments were in kind and the majority of people can hardly have touched money at all. But it was natural enough that, in so far as there was buying

[8] *Summa Theologica*, IIa IIae, Qu. 66, art. 2.
[9] *Summa Theologica*, IIa IIae, Qu. 76, art. 4.

and selling and the handling of money, it was quite alien to the medieval mind to leave such matters to the free play of the market. On the contrary, the men of the Middle Ages thought that there was a just price at which goods should exchange and a just wage by which labour should be remunerated. Above all, the lending of money at usury was sternly forbidden.

Our concern is not so much with the exposition of Thomist economic doctrines as with seeing what is their degree of authority. As we have seen, it was a series of accidents which had produced the medieval society—a society Catholic within itself and at the same time threatened with overthrow from without. Such a society was never at all envisaged by the early Christians. It was natural that men, finding themselves in such a society, should take measures of self-preservation—should consider what were the conditions which justified them in making war against the external enemy, what should be their policy towards the heretic at home. Whether they answered those questions correctly in detail is not for the moment the point. The point is that they were answering questions which had been forced on them by circumstances which did not exist at all for the early disciples—questions upon which there was therefore no direct guidance to be found in the recorded teaching of our Lord. On the other hand, it was clear that, though, while the Christians were a small minority, it might be possible to solve these problems by what might be called the method of generosity recommended by our Lord—by the Christian merely conceding any point in dispute, it being assumed that the other party was non-Christian—a more precise doctrine of what constituted a just title to money or property was required in a Christian society.

St Thomas and the medieval schoolmen condemned usury on the ground that in the practice of usury the lender appropriated something that was not his own. Money, they said, was sterile. If A lends B a pound, after a year has passed that pound is still a pound. If he compels B to repay him a guinea, then he has robbed B of a shilling. But, says the modern man, during the interval B has had the use of that pound. It is therefore reasonable that he should pay something for that use. The objection does not answer the schoolman's point. It is of course true that everybody has to eat every day, while many workers—he who is building a factory, he who is sowing the field, he who is mending the road—work on any given day on work which, it is hoped, will eventually add to society's wealth but which at the moment adds nothing. Therefore those who work on capital goods must by some device be fed by the rest of the community. This is obviously true whatever our form of society—whether we have capitalism or communism or any other system. Society cannot go on unless there is investment. St Thomas was well aware of this. He had no objection to a man investing in a project, taking the risk that the project would prove profitable, if it proved profitable, taking his share of the profits and, being prepared to lose his money, if it was a failure. For then he was robbing no one. He was not taking his profit from another. On the contrary as the result of the use of his money the world's wealth was increased and he was merely enjoying his share in that increase. It would be, as we have said, absurd to treat our Lord's parable of the talents as a mere essay in economics, but nevertheless it showed that he was well enough aware that people invested their money and had no objection to their doing so and to their making a profit out of doing so. He rather condemned them for not investing and not increasing their fortune. St Thomas did not object to risk capital any more than did our Lord. What he objected to was an arrangement where A would have the right to exact a payment of interest out of B whether B's use of the money had proved profitable or not. In modern parlance he would have objected to debenture shares but would not have objected to ordinary shares.

Now this teaching of St Thomas was derived not from any teaching of Christ but confessedly from the teaching of Aristotle. Aristotle and St Thomas were two of the greatest figures in history and it would be folly indeed not to pay attention to anything that they had to say. Modern economists, like Keynes, who were utterly without Catholic sympathies, have told us how they came to see that the medieval theory of usury contained an important truth and that the modern world might have been saved from much instability if it had remained mindful of it. Still, Aristotle did not speak from another world, revealing to us truths that were undiscoverable to the unaided intellect.

Nevertheless St Thomas' teaching on usury, if less than a dogma, was equally much more than the mere opinion of an economist. It was enforced on the faithful as a matter of sin. He who had been guilty of practising usury was barred from the sacraments until he had confessed and made restitution. Nor was the ban on usury merely a matter of discipline, like not eating meat on Friday, binding only on Catholics. In his letter to the Duchess of Brabant, *De Regimine Judaeorum*, St Thomas explains how the Jews within the Duchess' dominions who have practised usury have been guilty of robbing those on whom they have practised and must be compelled to surrender their gains—though he characteristically also explains that the fact that the Jews have no right to the money does not mean that the Duchess is entitled to seize it for herself. It must either be restored to its proper owners, or, if that should not prove possible, used for the public good.[10]

POST-REFORMATION DEVELOPMENTS

In the seventeenth century the discipline of the Church on usury was modified. The divinely revealed truth was that it was wrong to steal. The Church did not unsay that teaching nor could she have done so, but, after much debate and gradually, the decision was taken that circumstances had so changed that it was no longer possible to condemn as mortal sin some practices which would have been so condemned in the different circumstances of previous centuries. As long as the possessor of money normally kept his money in physical form and in store, then it was possible to argue

[10] *De Regimine Judaeorum. Ad Ducissam Brabantiae.*

with Aristotle that he who lent money to another was lending a commodity which would otherwise have been unemployed and that therefore, if he exacted interest on the repayment of that money, he was taking something for nothing and robbing his debtor. But with the great commercial developments of the sixteenth and seventeenth centuries consequent on the discovery of America and the beginnings of industrial production there was a new situation. By the seventeenth century he who found himself in possession of any surplus money would normally invest it directly or indirectly in some enterprise. If therefore a borrower asked him for the loan of some money, he was asking him to deny himself a chance of possible investment. The lender could say that he was losing a chance of gain—*lucrum cessans*—or incurring a loss—*damnum emergens*—and could therefore, argued the Church, legitimately demand payment for the sacrifice.

Critics—both inside and outside the Church—have been found to argue that the Church was in this new ruling abandoning a principle, or at the least making a virtue of necessity. Europe was by now divided. Plenty of people for their various enterprises wanted money and were prepared to pay interest for it. If Catholics would not lend them money at interest, then all that would happen would be that they would go to the Jews or the Protestants of Amsterdam, and the financial leadership of Europe would pass wholly out of Catholic hands. Or alternatively—and more probably—Catholic bankers, like the Fuggers of Augsburg, would defy the rulings of the Church rather than lose the whole of their business. It would be foolish to deny that the threat that power would pass into the hands of Protestant bankers and the threat that Catholic bankers would be disobedient, if an utterly rigid line was taken, were both present to the minds of the ecclesiastical authorities. Suarez is frank in admitting this as a relevant consideration. Those who condemn them without qualification for their flexibility do not always fully understand what was their problem. Lord Keynes, for instance, in the later years of his life often confessed his deep debt to medieval theories of usury. Whereas in his youth he and almost all other economists had been inclined to dismiss such theories as tiresomely fantastic and quite irrelevant to the problems of the modern world, in his later years he was more inclined to complain of the Church for having, as he thought, minimized the great truth which she had discovered. In a private letter, for instance, to Sir Cornelius Gregg, expressing his thanks for a gift of a copy of Fr Lewis Watt's book on Usury, Lord Keynes wrote:

> I am most grateful to you for sending me that little volume by Fr Watt. It is in my judgement extremely well done, clear, comprehensive and short. Much the best account of a very interesting subject from the Catholic point of view that I have ever read. Like you, I am rather worried that he has not kept the scholastic lingo, especially as the phrases *lucrum cessans* and *damnum emergens* do, as you say, bring out the point much better than any alternative phrase that he has introduced. In fact, the failure to use these old terms seems to me to have had the effect that he has not sufficiently high-lighted what clearly emerges from his argument and is indeed the essence of it, namely that the correct measure of the interest is the loss actual or potential to the lender and not the gain to the borrower. In other words it is usury to extract from the borrower some amount additional to the true sacrifice of the lender which the weakness of the borrower's position or his extremity of need happens to make a feasible proposition. I find it interesting to put it in this way because it really amounts to exactly the same thing as my theory of liquidity preference.[11]

Yet of course an economist like Lord Keynes may properly debate whether it would be for the advantage of society to have laws forbidding usury. It is his business to decide which is the system which will give society the greatest economic prosperity. But that is not the business of the ecclesiastical authorities. Their concern, in so far as they are giving definite rulings, is rather to decide what practices are so evil, so plainly contrary to the moral law, that they can declare anyone who indulges in them to be guilty of mortal sin. A pope or bishop

11 *The Tablet*, December 26th, 1959.

who declared some practice to be a mortal sin when it was
evident that it was not a mortal sin would himself be guilty
of grave sin. The Church never said that it was desirable that
people should lend money at interest. She never in any way
reproved anyone who for his conscience's sake refused to
make such a use of his money. She merely refused any longer to
take the responsibility of saying that he who did so necessarily
committed a mortal sin.

The seventeenth century in fact saw the transition from a
second to a third phase in the Church's history in its relation
to economic problems. In the first phase—in the first centuries
of our era—as we have said, there was no question of
Christianity being sufficiently important to influence legislation. The only question was, Which of the laws of the pagan
state should Christians obey? The second phase of a thousand
years—the years of the Dark Ages and the Middle Ages—
was one during which, largely through accident and without
premeditation, Catholics lived in a Catholic society which was
itself under attack from without. Whether it was a good thing
that society should be of that nature was debatable, but,
granted that it was so, it obviously compelled the Church to
offer a much more positive teaching as to what sort of economic
and other social arrangements were desirable. The notion that
a society in order to survive must necessarily be united in
religion had so fully captured men's minds that, when the
conflict of the Reformation first broke out, there was, to begin
with, no question on either side but that it must be fought out
until there was a total victory for one side or the other. The
Calvinists had as firm an ambition to make Europe all Calvinist as had the Catholics to make it once again all Catholic.
But it proved in the end that neither side was strong enough
wholly to destroy the other. The Hundred Years' War of
Religion therefore ended in a compromise—a compromise of
partial toleration. The individual was to some very limited
extent allowed to make a personal choice of his religion. But
in general each sovereign settled what should be the religion
of his realm.

The formula in which this policy was expressed was *Cuius regio eius religio*. The nations of Europe divided themselves into Catholic nations and Protestant nations. The vast majority of Catholics lived in Catholic States and of Protestants lived in Protestant States, and it was accepted that anyone who was so obstinate as to insist on professing a religion different from that of his ruler must expect to have to submit to stringent disabilities. The few Catholics who were living in Protestant States could not expect to influence the legislation of those States. In fact there were harsh penal laws passed to make certain that they did not influence it. Thus we get a third phase in the Church's history—the phase in which the great majority of Catholics indeed still lived in Catholic countries but in which the great economic developments by which the face of society was being reshaped were predominantly taking place in Protestant countries where the Catholics could not hope to exercise any influence.

CHAPTER II

THE CHURCH AND NINETEENTH-CENTURY ECONOMICS

BEFORE RERUM NOVARUM

The third phase—the phase in which Catholics lived predominantly in Catholic countries and in which the small minority of Catholics in Protestant countries asked for and received in gradual and grudging stages varying degrees of toleration—lasted from the middle of the seventeenth to the middle of the nineteenth centuries. Catholic policy in Catholic countries was to demand the recognition of Catholicism as the religion of the State and to attach considerable importance to that recognition. There were conflicts even in Catholic countries between Church and State as the absolute monarch threatened the Church's rights—Gallicanism in France, Josephism in Austria, the rule of the *rois philosophes* in Spain and other smaller countries. The great French Revolution attacked all established institutions, and the Church among them, in the name of liberty, fraternity and equality, and an attempt was made to impose upon the Church a constitutional system. It failed. Napoleon temporarily composed the quarrel of the Revolution and the Church by the Concordat, but it was a fragile settlement and the quarrel soon broke out again. After Napoleon's defeat it was a debatable question whether it was desirable to restore the pope to his temporal dominions. There was much to be said for taking advantage of the opportunity of freeing him from those entanglements. However, largely on the insistence of the great Protestant Powers, Britain and Prussia, it was decided, on the general principle that the map, wherever possible, must be restored exactly as it was in 1789, that the Temporal Power should be restored. This of course led to many complications when the Italian nationalist movement started to demand a united Italian State—a State of which, had it not been for the pope's position, Rome was the inevitable capital. The Vatican's political policy was, up till 1870, dominated by this problem of the Temporal Power, and it was not until the Temporal Power was lost that it was free to turn its attention to the economic problems of the day.

The medieval economy had been essentially an agricultural economy. To it the town-dweller was an exception and medieval economic theory, whether religious or secular, never quite made up its mind where to fit him in. The growth of the towns in the sixteenth century created a new economic pattern, and the first thinker, I fancy, to try explicitly to define the place of the city and the town-dweller within the new economy was Giovanni Botero, who wrote his *Treatise Concerning the Causes of the Magnificence and Greatness of Cities* in the early years of the seventeenth century.[1] The two hundred years from the middle of the seventeenth to the middle of the nineteenth centuries had been years of progress. New inventions, following quickly on one another as what is known as the Industrial Revolution developed, had steadily increased society's volume of production. On the other hand, property and power were often in the hands of ruthless men. In the name of increased productivity they did not hesitate to abolish privileges where those privileges were in the hands of persons other than themselves. In France the feudal lords had been allowed by Richelieu to keep their privileges over the peasants but had been stripped of their powers and freed

[1] Giovanni Botero (1540–1617).

from the obligations of military service. They continued to exact their privileges until deprived of them by the French Revolution. The French Revolution left the agricultural land in the hands of the peasants and industrial production in the hands of the capitalists who, under a formula of liberalism, denied the right of the State to interfere with their total freedom to do what they liked with their own. Under the rule of Louis Philippe the political régime of France was not one likely to attend much to papal pronouncements on economics even had such been forthcoming.

There was of course even less chance of attention being paid to the pope in England, the main home during those years of industrial development. In England the landlords of the eighteenth century had ruthlessly enclosed the common lands, which had been traditionally the property of the villagers, in the name of more efficient production and the countryside was left with a population of landless agricultural workers. The surplus of that population drifted off into the towns where it provided the labour by which the factories of the new industrial revolution were built and worked. Traditional organizations of local or craft self-government, such as the guilds, were suppressed and in the early years of the Industrial Revolution savage measures were taken by Government against any new organizations such as those of trade unions, into which the workers might attempt to band themselves for mutual protection.

The teaching of St Thomas, enunciated in a society that was predominantly agricultural, obviously required at least restatement in this new world. On the other hand, while the major developments of the new world were taking place in countries where the Catholics were but a minute minority, the popes could hardly hope that any restatement of Catholic teaching would have a large influence on the immediate development of society. What should they do? It is perhaps fair to say that up till the middle of the nineteenth century papal policy on economic matters had been content to give rulings and, if the rulings were neglected, to protest. As the Industrial Revolution was taking place in a Protestant country where manifestly no attention would be paid to papal rulings, the papacy did not attempt to lay down positive Catholic teaching on the problems of industrialism. Catholics were left with little guidance save to relieve by works of charity such distress as came their personal way. This many Catholics most notably did and the nineteenth century is a century most nobly full of Catholic charitable work, but there was throughout the bulk of the century little attempt to lay down a Catholic economic policy.

In the first half of the century there had indeed been a movement in France which advocated that the Church should support the cause of democracy, but conservative influence within the Church and anti-clerical influences within the democratic parties were too strong. The complication of the Temporal Power perhaps made it inevitable that the Church should be suspicious of the new rising force of nationalism. The French Democratic Catholic movement therefore failed. Pius IX at his accession in 1846 attempted to introduce constitutional rule into Rome. That was an even more disastrous failure and by the middle of the century the Church appeared to most judges, inevitably perhaps, as an essentially conservative institution. In the economic field she had sponsored certain positive works as, for instance, the founding of savings banks, but it was perhaps hardly surprising that the new revolutionary economists—Proudhon, Marx, Bakunin and the like—should have paid little attention to these and should have seen the Church as an upholder of the established order and therefore as an enemy to be attacked. In England, it is true, many of the social reformers were less hostile to religion and often enough invoked the name of Christ in support of their policies. But the Christianity which these reformers preached was an entirely Protestant Christianity and it would have never occurred to them that they had any lessons to learn from the Catholic Church. That being so, even if the Church had had no quarrel with the new revolutionary doctrines on economic grounds, the papacy must necessarily have been apprehensive at the growth of that movement, nor was it to be expected that Catholics should be allowed to join such patently anti-Catholic societies as the Carbonari or the Freemasons. But the greater the need of dissociating the Church from irreligious movements and philosophies, the greater the importance of showing that the Church's policy was not therefore one of merely negative conservatism. Clearly there was a social problem on which Catholics ought to have something to say.

It was under the papacy of Leo XIII, who succeeded Pius IX in 1878, and was therefore the first pope not to be encumbered with the tasks of the Temporal Power, that problems of a positive Catholic economic policy were first frankly debated. It was difficult for Catholics to say much in Europe because of the close relations there of Church and State. It was difficult for them to say much in England because they were so few and uninfluential. But in the United States there was now owing to immigration, mainly Irish, a sizeable Catholic minority. There was also a tradition of free speech, of the separation of Church and State and of non-confessional organizations. There was an opportunity for Catholics there such as they did not enjoy in any other country.

There was in the United States an organization known as the Knights of Labor, the forerunner of the American Federation of Labor, which had no anti-Catholic bias and in which there was no reason why Catholics should not play their part. Its president was a Catholic, Terence Powderly. Careful as it was to avoid all policies of violence or conspiracy, yet, as was natural in the temper of the times, it did not escape attack either from Catholics or from non-Catholics. A somewhat similar organization in Canada was rebuked from Rome at the instigation of the Archbishop of Quebec and, had it not been for Cardinal Gibbons' vigorous intervention on behalf of the Knights of Labor, they might not have received the approbation of Leo XIII. Cardinal Gibbons wrote to Leo to point out that the Catholic working man nobly refused to join the Freemasons in spite of the considerable material advantage in doing so: "Our working men join associations in no way in conflict with religion," he wrote, "seeking nothing but mutual protection and help and the legitimate assertion of their rights. Must they also find themselves threatened with condemnation, hindered from their only means of self-defence?''

The pope not only supported the Knights of Labor in America, but, in spite of the less favourable atmosphere for Catholic Action in Europe than in America, he started the custom of receiving deputations of workers which came to him from European countries. These deputations came mainly from France under the leadership of Count Albert de Mun and Léon Harmel, a noted Catholic employer. In Italy itself the Catholic congresses were at first mainly occupied with the political question of the relation of Church and State, but with the fourth such Congress at Bergamo, in 1877, social questions were on the agenda and the eighth Congress at Lucca in 1887 sponsored a programme for the introduction of guild constitutions into industry.

The closing years of Pius' reign had been filled with the conflict between Bismarck and the German Catholics known as the Kulturkampf. The battle had been on political rather than on economic issues and its details are therefore beyond our concern. After Leo's accession it was settled by the compromise of 1886 and thenceforward the German Government was anxious that its relations with the Catholics and with the Catholic political party, the Centre party, should be as friendly as possible. It needed the votes of the Centre in support of its military programmes. There was a large field of common ground between the Church and the German State in economic matters. Both were anxious to check the growing power of Socialism and both thought that that power could not be checked by mere repression but only by a positive alternative social policy. Catholic workers' organizations were at that time stronger in Germany than in any other country, having been brought into being largely by the work of Bishop Ketteler of Mainz, whose *Christianity and the Labour Question*, published in 1864, was a pioneer work in that field. Therefore when the new Kaiser, the young William II, in 1890 summoned an international conference at Berlin to discuss industrial legislation, he was anxious that Pope Leo should be associated with that conference. He wrote to him to ask for his cooperation on the ground that the Pope had "always used his influence in favour of the poor and forsaken of human society". Leo, though not seeing his way to send a personal representative, expressed his satisfaction that the Prince-Bishop of Breslau was to attend. From England, Cardinal Manning wrote to congratulate the pope on his initiative. Manning of course for many years before the publication of *Rerum Novarum* had been prominent in social work and had intervened most dramatically in the great London Dock strike of 1889. Cardinal Moran in Australia had similarly thrown his influence on to the side of the workers in the great Sydney strike of 1890.

LEO XIII AND RERUM NOVARUM

Thus, already in the 1880's, there was plenty of understanding in the Catholic world that we had moved into a new age with its new problems upon which the Church must take her stand. There was in all countries plenty of Catholic interest in social and economic problems, but that interest was in general least in the purely Catholic countries and most in the countries where Catholics lived side by side with their non-Catholic fellow citizens. But, as was only to be expected in view of the Church's conservative record over the previous half century, while some were insisting that false economic doctrines could only be countered by the preaching of true economic doctrines, others—monarchists in France, capitalists in America and elsewhere—were denouncing all such teaching as compromises with evil and as attempts to sup with the devil with an insufficiently long spoon, that must necessarily end in disaster. Heresies such as Americanism and Modernism were in the air. Some of those who were infected with these heresies were also favourers of the new social doctrines. Critics were found to argue that the connection was not fortuitous. Leo XIII did not greatly like the phrase Christian Democracy which the favourers of social reform had coined. Indeed it nowhere appears in *Rerum Novarum* and is not to be found in a papal document before *Graves de Communi* published in 1901. But, whatever the phraseology that he might choose, it was inevitable, if serious dissension within the Catholic body was to be avoided, that the pope should indicate clearly whether the mind of the Church was merely conservative or whether it was in favour of social reform. For this reason among others Leo XIII issued *Rerum Novarum* on May 15th, 1891.

In this new world the old weapons of order, excommunication and denunciation of mortal sin might be effective in recalling an individual Catholic to right conduct—or they might not. But they could no longer be of much effect in changing the pattern of society, for that pattern was not being made to any important extent by Catholics. On the other hand if the pope was to say his say on the evils of the day, recommending remedies for the most part not so much by an appeal to the Church's authority as on their own intrinsic merits, basing his argument, as far as possible, on moral principles which Protestants, and perhaps even non-believers of good will, would share with Catholics, it was not hopeless to expect that some attention would be paid to what he said.

Rerum Novarum, then, begins with a description of the economic crisis of the day. The development of industrialism, the destruction in the name of free competition of the workers' traditional organizations such as the guilds, had created a situation in which the total production of society was indeed greatly increased but in which wealth and power were to an inordinate extent concentrated into a few hands. Leo XIII describes this situation in vigorous language, in language which to many of the complacent Liberals of that day seemed exaggerated. "The hiring of labour", he writes, "and the conduct of trade are concentrated in the hands of a comparatively few, so that a small number of very rich men have been able to lay upon the masses of the labouring poor a yoke little better than that of slavery itself."

Having denounced the evil in such forthright terms, the pope then turns to consider the suggested remedies of it.   He takes first the Socialist solution and rejects it. He uses "Socialism" to mean a system under which private property would be entirely abolished. This, he says, would bring no remedy and would in itself be unjust, since it would deprive man of property to which he has a natural right. The workers would, he argues, be the worst sufferers, since the deepest and most natural ambition of every man is to obtain for himself a little property. The evil of the economy was that there were too many people who did not possess any property. It would be no remedy to deprive everybody of property. The fundamental institution was not the State but the family, and the very existence of the family, with its obligation on the parents to support their children, implies the existence of private property. The State has indeed a right and a duty to step in to prevent exceptional distress or a right to protect children against abnormal and unnatural parents, who neglect them or treat them with sadistic cruelty. But normally it is the duty of parents to bring up their children and it is only in the exceptional case that the State has the right to interfere with their manner of doing so. There was, said the pope, "a fundamental principle . . . of the inviolability of private property". Inequalities of income were inevitable and not in themselves to be condemned. Suffering was the necessary consequence of the Fall and it was both futile and blasphemous to complain of it. Therefore Leo unhesitatingly condemns theories of class warfare and rebukes those agitators who preach it. The employer who breaks his contract or defrauds labourers of their wage is indeed guilty of one of the gravest of all sins, but to employ labour is not in itself a sin.

The critic is obviously tempted to intervene at some point such as this and to ask to what practical conclusion all this leads. The pope, he is likely to say, begins with a denunciation of the present system in language that will seem to many exaggerated. He denounces the distribution of property, in which so much property is concentrated into a very few hands and so many have none at all, by comparing it to "slavery". The stickler for verbal exactitude might well say that this is rhetoric—that the situation may indeed contain great evils but that slavery is an exact word and that, where there is payment in cash, where a man has a right—if sometimes little more than a theoretical right—to change his employment and to spend his leisure time as he wishes, that is not slavery. But in any event, the critic would continue, granted that these are grave evils in the present system by whatever name we call them, how does the pope propose that they be remedied? He rejects the Socialist remedy. He says that there is an "inalienable" right to private property. The amount of land is limited. If some by definition have too much and if nevertheless justice forbids one from taking away from those who have too much, where are we to find the property with which those who now have none can equip themselves?

The pope begins his answer to this criticism by restating the Thomist doctrine of property. The rich indeed have a right to their own but they have not a right to do as they like with their own. There should indeed be a redistribution of property but it should come about not through the compulsory action of the State but through the voluntary surrender by the rich. It is true that the State cannot compel the rich to give alms but that by no means implies that the rich man is morally free to give alms or not according to his whim. He is under a positive obligation, binding under sin, to give away his superfluity. "The rich should tremble at the threatenings of Jesus Christ," writes the pope. "A most strict account must be given to the Supreme Judge for all we possess." It is one thing to have a right to the possession of money and another to have a right to use money as one wills. He quotes from St Thomas, "Man should not consider his material possessions as his own but as common to all, so as to share them without hesitation when others are in need". He echoed the teaching of Bossuet that that the Church is "eminently" the Church of the poor and that the only title of the rich to be admitted into it derives from the relief that they give to the poor.

This, again the critic may say, is a counsel of perfection. If the rich should all behave in this very edifying fashion, a utopia would perhaps be achieved—though those who possess a superfluity have a duty to invest as well as a duty to give away—but what are the poor supposed to do if the rich do not behave thus? The pope reminds us of the achievement of the Church—of the works of charity which the Church has organized and with which she has infused society. The Church is not concerned with the soul alone, he argues. Christianity was the religion of God made Man—of the Incarnate Son who broke bread and ate it. Man has his material needs. He has a right to satisfy them. We are all members one of another. "When you did it to one of the least of my brethren here, you did it to me" (Matt. 25. 40). We have a duty to see that our neighbour can satisfy his material needs as well as we ourselves. The pope reminds us of the work that the Church has done from apostolic times onwards to relieve the needy.

Yet the obstinate questionings remain. Though it may be the will of God that the rich should give of their super-abundance to the poor, it is obviously uncertain how far they will do so even in a purely Catholic society—and Leo was addressing a world which was largely non-Catholic and where overwhelmingly the greater part of large industrial enter-prises were in non-Catholic hands. If the secular state took no action very little would happen. Of this he was well aware. Therefore he insisted that, in supplement to private charity, the State must play its part. The State has of course in the first place the duty to maintain law and order. It has the duty to ensure the freedom of religious practice. It has the duty to enforce contracts. Beyond that it is wrong that anyone should have to live under conditions inimical to health. The State has a duty to insist on the preservation of at least such minimum standards of housing, sanitation and conditions of labour that health does not suffer. If the general convenience of society is threatened by strikes or lockouts, the State has a duty to step in and to prevent the parties to an industrial dispute from carrying on that dispute in such a way as to damage that general convenience. The burden of proof rests on the State whenever it seeks to interfere in the personal lives of its citizens. "The law," writes the pope, "must not undertake more, nor proceed further, than is required for the remedy of the evil or the removal of the mischief." Nevertheless, when there is an evil or a mischief, it is the duty of the State to interfere and it has no right to evade its responsibility by invoking some pretended dogma of *laissez-faire*.

If the State has a general duty to interfere it has a special duty to interfere to protect the poor, since obviously the poor man, being the weaker party, is likely, if unassisted, to get the worse of a bargain with the rich. If it prevents a strike because of the general inconvenience which a strike would cause, then it has a duty to examine the grievances for which the strike was threatened and, where it finds them just, to insist on their remedy. It has a right to insist on conditions of employment which allow the worker a reasonable amount of leisure, to forbid conditions which are damaging to health and physique, particularly for women and children. Above all in uncontrolled bargaining the capitalist with resources behind him will often be at a great advantage over the worker without resources and without alternative employment, who has no choice but to accept the conditions that are offered to him, however unjust. Therefore, the State has a duty to insist on a living and a just wage—to prescribe a minimum sufficient to keep the worker and his family in modest comfort—and to make it a penal offence that wages below that minimum should be offered. Though there is nothing intrinsically immoral in a wage system and in the employer-employee relationship, what is desirable, wherever it is possible, is that the head of a family should himself be a property-owner. He then has behind him some resources, however slender, and is therefore in a better position to drive an equitable bargain with his employer.

In agriculture direct ownership of property on a wide scale is desirable and, whatever the arguments in favour of larger units in the name of efficiency, the pope preferred the small unit. In industry and in agriculture alike, where combination is necessary, it should, if possible, be on a cooperative basis as between equal partners, rather than imposed by a master on his servants or employees. He deplores the destruction of the old guilds and asserts the right of the workers to put in their place new organizations of their own for their own protection, such as trade unions. The State has the duty to recognize and protect such organizations. Only through such organizations can the worker be strong enough to strike a fair bargain with his employer. "A brother that is helped by his brother is like a strong city," he quotes from Proverbs. On the other hand he recognizes the possibility that such organizations may behave in their turn in tyrannical or subversive fashion. If they should do so, if they should be found to be using their power not to protect one another but to dominate society or to subvert its fundamental institutions, if they should be found to be exercising compulsion on individual workers, then it may be the duty of the workers to refuse obedience to an existing organization and to set up a rival organization to fight against it for the fundamental rights of men.

The State, says the pope, has no right to forbid these "private societies" as he calls them—these organizations formed by citizens for themselves. For "to enter into a society of this kind is the natural right of man. . . . If it [the State] forbids its citizens to form associations, it contradicts the very principle of its own existence." The State is only justified in dissolving an association if it proves itself evidently hostile to society. "Every precaution should be taken not to violate the rights of individuals and not to impose unreasonable regulations under pretence of public benefit." The encyclical also includes paragraphs on specifically Catholic associations within the Church. These, though doubtless in themselves of great importance, are not within our direct concern at the moment, where we are discussing Catholic teaching on economic matters.

It is, I think, clear enough how Leo had it in mind that he

would meet the fundamental dilemma. How can we increase the property of the poor if we are not going to take property from the rich? Cardinal Cajetan, the sixteenth-century Thomist philosopher and antagonist of Luther, had put forward a proposition that perilously resembled the Wycliffian proposition that all dominion was founded on grace. In his commentary on St Thomas he had argued that the State—the judge—had the right and duty to take away from the rich man such of his wealth as he did not spend on the relief of the poor. Even if we suppose a purely Catholic society in which both rich and poor and the judge himself are all Catholic such a principle is hardly acceptable. The chaos that would be caused by the attempt to apply it is clear enough. The Church may say to the rich but wicked man, "Your soul is in peril if you do not make a better use of your riches," but the State—the judge—has no means of judging the secret places of the heart. How is a magistrate to give his ruling that one man is using his wealth well and another is using it ill? It is clear that the attempt to apply such a principle would cause enormously more evils than it remedied. Therefore Leo was clearly right in refusing Cajetan's remedy.

St Thomas, writing in a purely Catholic society, had argued that the rich man ought to surrender his superfluity. He was bound to do it under pain of sin from the Church. He never said that it was the duty of the State to take it from him. Admittedly St Thomas' teaching would have less practical effect in a society largely secularist than in St Thomas' society when all men went in fear of the Church's condemnation. Yet Cajetan's remedy is no remedy. The economy of the nineteenth century differed from the economy of St Thomas' day in another way. It was an economy of invention. In the Middle Ages methods of production remained substantially the same from generation to generation and therefore there was no notable increase in the total product. In the nineteenth century methods were being daily improved and the total product therefore increased. Leo envisages expanding industries in which it will be possible to give new shares to the workers without taking old shares away from the existing owners. He teaches that there is an inalienable right to property. The State has no right to take away an owner's property, but that does not mean that an owner has in the past necessarily been justified in every use that he made of his property, and the State may well be justified in saying to an old-fashioned owner or landlord, who had been in the habit of riding roughshod over tenants or workers, that he may indeed keep his property but that he shall no longer be permitted to take advantage of his ownership of property to deny to others their fundamental human rights.

CATHOLICS AND RERUM NOVARUM

One sometimes comes across Catholics who argue that, if only all the world were Catholic, the precepts of the encyclical might well be put into practice but that, with things as they are, in our modern mixed and secularized societies, there is little that we can do about it. We can, they say, in practice, only do as the world does. It is a defeatist, and indeed often an almost dishonest, line of argument. For, if we look at such predominantly Catholic societies as still exist—in Malta, or Spain, or Ireland, or French Canada—we cannot honestly pretend that their entire population is filled with a knowledge of the encyclical or with the determination to apply it. It cannot even be pretended that the encyclical has been the universal and evident inspiration of the policy of the Catholic party in Italy. No one can see in the social conditions of Naples and Sicily today an ideal example of the application of Christian social principles. On the contrary, the encyclical has clearly been most studied in countries where the Catholics are but a minority of the population—in Germany, France, Holland and to some extent in Britain and the United States— where the Catholics have to meet the challenge of opposition, and even in those countries some of its most enthusiastic champions have been found among non-Catholics. Belgium is perhaps the only country where almost all those who profess a religion profess the Catholic religion and where at the same time there is widespread interest in Catholic social teaching.

There is no paradox in this that it is among mixed populations that the largest interest in such teaching is generally found. For with our century we passed into a fourth phase in the Church's history—the phase where the typical Catholic is no longer as in former centuries to be found in the so-called Catholic countries—where there are few countries which possess a wholly Catholic population and where little encouragement is given to political measures to keep the whole population nominally conformist. The typical Catholic of the twentieth century is a member of a society, the greater number of whose members are not Catholic and in which he cannot expect to receive any special privileges or more than toleration from the law. In such a society it would be fatuous were the Catholic merely to throw his hands up in despair and exclaim, "If only this were a Catholic country, what things we could do! As it is, we can do nothing." On the contrary, the Catholic must play his full part in such a society, must co-operate with his fellow non-Catholics in all things save *communicatio in sacris* and must discover how much of a common cause he has with his fellow non-Catholics of good will.

Therefore, the greater part of Leo XIII's economic teaching does not in any way rest exclusively on revealed truth. His appeals to specific Catholic doctrine are few. The greater part of the argument is based on natural morality—not to say, on common sense—and there is no reason why a non-Catholic should not be as appreciative of it as a Catholic. Indeed it is a commonplace today that the theory which sees all history as a relentless war between the capitalist and the workers is a monomaniac's folly. Even if we look solely to immediate happiness, it is clear that, while indeed, as Leo XIII insists, man has his material needs and cannot normally be happy if he is compelled to live in a condition of intolerable insecurity and poverty, yet a law of diminishing returns in the relation of wealth to happiness rapidly sets in, and experience gives us little reason to think that the rich are happier, just as it gives us little reason to think that they are more virtuous, than those of moderate means. One cannot but feel that there is a lack of balance in the politicians, whether they be of the right or of the left, who hold out as the object of policy a doubling of the standard of living within a generation without any detailed explanation what they mean by a doubled standard.

There are indeed material problems still to be solved in the world, but to make two television sets grow where one grows today is hardly sane. Since most men are blind to the particular madnesses of their own day, the worship of continuous material progress appears to them as common sense in opposition to the so-called idealism of religious teaching, but to a future age, if future age there is to be, it will, we may be certain, appear as unbalanced as any of the extravagant heresies of early Christian or of medieval times. We need not react from gross materialism to an extreme asceticism nor frown upon a reasonable indulgence in cakes and ale. Let us find means of increasing wealth in the directions in which there is some purpose in increasing it, but let us always insist that there be a purpose in our activity before we undertake it. The mere worship of progress and activity as in itself necessarily good is hardly sane, nor would man have ever come to think of it as sane had not the decay of religion left a void in his soul which, like the empty house that was swept and garnished in the Gospels, must be filled with something because, as Chesterton said, "Men who will not believe in God will believe in anything". It has always been the wisdom of the Church to ordain holidays from time to time and he who neglects that wisdom neglects it at his peril.

That is, I suppose, the explanation of the difficult parable of the unjust steward. Our Lord was a great satirist. He did not believe that even on materialistic standards any purpose was served by merely juggling with book entries or that in that way the wealth of the world was increased. But that is what materialistic people do believe in a materialistic age. It is such an age that permits bankers to create credit by a stroke of the pen and to obtain such power that—to quote Pius XI in *Quadragesimo Anno*—"none dare breathe against their will". The unjust steward, if he was going to be a worldly man, was wise to indulge in such tricks, for these are the tricks which the Mammon of Iniquity understands and they will feel more comfortable in the company of stewards who indulge in them. There is an infinite pity in the concluding sentence of the Gospel account of the parable: "And the Lord commended the unjust steward." He had compassion on the world of children, who are the masters of money, even as at another time he had compassion on the multitude. *La miséricorde de Dieu est infinie. Il sauvera même un riche.*

The most definite teaching of the Church about economics is her protest against all theories which admit only economic values—alike against theories of economic determinism on the left and against the economic man, exclusively engaged upon buying in cheapest and selling in dearest markets, of the classical economists. The Catholic tradition insists upon the "two swords"—the two authorities of Church and State—and it has been throughout Christian history the first concern of the Church to safeguard her independence, economic and otherwise, of the State. The Philosopher Kings of the eighteenth century and the masters of the Revolution had claimed—and to some extent obtained—inordinate power for the State over the Church. Leo's strong opposition to what he called Socialism and his championship of widely distributed property and subsidiary societies was not therefore fundamentally for the economic reason that an economy that was not over-centralized was likely to be more efficient and to produce more —though that was in itself a plausible enough opinion—so much as for the moral reason that a too strong State was a threat alike to the Church and to liberty. It was an anxiety that to many seemed exaggerated in 1891. Few will think it exaggerated today.

Perhaps a criticism that some will make of *Rerum Novarum* is that it does not say anything very striking. In its deter-

mination to preserve the balance, we may be told, it is almost
platitudinous. There are, I think, two answers to that. In the
first place, the pope was neither a politician nor a journalist.
He wrote for the ages—not for tomorrow's headlines—and
the Catholic way is the middle way, the way of moderation,
of balance, of the Aristotelian mean. Nor was it his intention,
any more than it is the purpose of the Church, to solve all
questions for us or to give us all the answers. She rather
presents us with a challenge. She tells us, as I have said, what
questions we ought to ask. She not only allows us but orders
us to discover the facts for ourselves, to exercise our own
judgement, indeed to differ among ourselves, to argue it out,
to decide where the balance of right policy lies. On the vast
majority of economic questions there is not a Catholic answer.
There are only Catholic questions. Secondly, we must remember that the date of *Rerum Novarum* was 1891. Between
1891 and today new and evil forces at which Leo and his contemporaries could not have guessed have arisen in the world.
On the other hand, there have been social developments,
some of which have strikingly corresponded with what Leo
advocated. Today those who accept democracy take for granted
the existence of trade unions. There are some indeed who
would argue that trade unions are today not too weak but too
strong—that they are to be criticized because they have sometimes gone beyond their proper function of safeguarding the
workers' rights and have been tyrannical in their treatment of
dissidents. Yet, whether or not there be justice in such
criticisms in particular cases, no responsible believer in
democracy today denies the right of workers to organize
themselves in strong and independent trade unions. The
desirability of a wide distribution of property is today generally
admitted. Even the Conservative party of Great Britain, for
instance—a party quite innocent of any Catholic sympathies—
has adopted the slogan of "a property-owning democracy,"
and similar gospels have been preached by various groups in
other countries.

It is true that, alike in Britain and in these other countries, it has been found a great deal easier to proclaim such a purpose than to discover a way of carrying it out. Still, the proclamation of the purpose is today familiar. Or again, in industry, thinkers like Mr Peter Drucker, and indeed many others, have proclaimed the necessity of finding means to make the workers feel that they "belong" to the industry for which they work. Schemes of profit-sharing and co-partnership in industry are today familiar, if again not always successful. Of them it is the Liberal party in Great Britain which has been the especial champion. Moderate Socialists angrily repudiate as a libel the notion that they see in nationalization a universal panacea of all ills. Some impatient people, reading *Rerum Novarum* today, might almost exclaim, "Well, we all agree with all that". It is only fair to remember that what seems a platitude in 1960 was by no means neces-sarily a platitude in 1891—that at that earlier date there were still many confident capitalist believers in *laissez-faire* to whom the advocacy of a trade union was "socialism" and schemes of identification of the workers with industry were "idealistic nonsense".

Yet, if things have in so many ways moved in the direction which Leo advocated, we must not exaggerate the extent to which they have so moved because of his advocacy. We need not be so pessimistic as to say that he has had no influence. In France and perhaps, above all, in Belgium, that would certainly be untrue. But it would not be easy to cite any evidence to show that any of the statesmen of Britain or America who have introduced the various measures of social reform over the last fifty years had any intimate acquaintance —or indeed any acquaintance at all—with the pope's encyclical. These measures have been overwhelmingly the work of men nourished in a Protestant tradition and for the most part singularly indefinite in their own religious beliefs. The British Socialists for instance in the 1959 election entitled one of their policy statements "Members One Of Another". It was noted that these words were a quotation from the Epistle of the Ephesians, but I do not know that any journalist noticed that they were a quotation that had been used by Pius XI in *Quadragesimo Anno*. Leo's rôle then has been not so much that of a prophet of the Old Testament—of a man who led the people along the way that they should go—as of a prophet in the sense of a man who foresaw the way that they must inevitably go, if they were not to perish. They have done not so much what he said that they should do as what he said that they would do.

CHAPTER III

PIUS XI

Ten years after *Rerum Novarum*, in 1901, Leo issued a further encyclical *Graves de Communi* which was, as it were, a progress report on it. It was perhaps mainly notable in that it marked, as has already been said, the first papal acceptance of the term Christian Democracy. The pope, having advised the French Catholics to accept the Republic and having advised the Catholics to support social reform, could not well object to Catholics, if they so wished, calling themselves Christian Democrats. But in general *Graves de Communi* is concerned with a summary of the progress that had been made towards the fulfilment of the pope's economic ideals alike among Catholics and among non-Catholics. Leo died in 1903 and was succeeded by Pius X. Pius X in the early years of his reign issued a *Motu Proprio* in which he explained that, while individual Catholics might call themselves Christian Democrats, it was not desirable to form Christian Democratic political parties. However, in face of the progress of Socialism it was becoming increasingly clear that there was little hope of Leo's principles being accepted unless Catholics, whether as individuals or as a political party, were allowed to vote. Therefore throughout the first two decades of the century the bans on Catholic participation in Italian political life were steadily being lifted until in 1919 Benedict XV withdrew the non-expedit which had compelled Catholics to be "neither elected nor electors" to the Italian Parliament. As a result a substantial Catholic party—the Partito Populare under the leadership of a priest, Don Luigi Sturzo—was returned as one

of the main parties in the Italian Chamber. In 1922 the Partito
Populare became the Chamber's most powerful party. Don
Sturzo, had he ever attained power, would certainly have
attempted to introduce the economic policies of Leo. Unfor-
tunately the cancellation of the non-expedit came too late to
save the Italian Parliamentary system.

QUADRAGESIMO ANNO

Forty years after *Rerum Novarum*, in 1931, Pius XI com-
memorated its anniversary by issuing the encyclical *Quadragesimo Anno* on "reconstructing the social order and perfecting
it conformably to the precepts of the Gospel". Its first task,
legitimately enough, was to show the world how prophetical
a document *Rerum Novarum* had proved itself—how much
more farseeing Leo XIII had shown himself to be than his
contemporaries in his diagnosis of the problems of the age.
Popes, like secular princes, use the royal We. In their case it
is by no means an empty form. It is a reminder that it is not
only the present occupant of the papal throne who is speaking
but that his voice is also the voice of the whole line of popes
from Peter onwards. It is therefore natural enough that, when
a pope treats of a subject that has already been treated by one
of his predecessors, be begins by recalling and reaffirming
what his predecessors have said. Never can such a technique
have been more manifestly appropriate than in *Quadragesimo
Anno*—written, as is shown by its very title, to recall to men's
mind Leo's *Rerum Novarum*. The second encyclical therefore
begins with a recapitulation. Yet many things had happened
between 1891 and 1931—a world war, a Communist revolution
in Russia, a Fascist revolution in Italy, developments in industrial relations—and Pius' task was not merely to repeat but to
interpret Leo's teaching in the light of changed circumstances.
Pius XI begins by summarizing the extent to which between
1891 and 1931 the world had moved in the direction which
Leo had advocated. Some may perhaps think that he somewhat
exaggerates the direct influence of Leo upon these changes
or indeed the part played in them by Catholic leaders. Yet he

is certainly justified in saying that it is to Leo more than to
any other modern man that we owe such recognition as there
is that the Church has lessons to teach on economic problems.
From the seventeenth century until Leo's pontificate the
Church had had little new to say on these problems and the
world had come to forget that she had an effective voice. "The
doctrine of *Rerum Novarum*," writes Pius XI, "began little by
little to penetrate among those also who, being outside
Catholic unity, do not recognize the authority of the Church;
and thus Catholic principles of sociology gradually became
part of the intellectual heritage of the human race."

Pius calls attention to the volume of social legislation in all
countries and to the growth of trade unions between 1891 and
1931. He discusses the question whether there should be
especial confessional trade unions. In a country in which
Catholics are in a minority and in which Catholic workers may
be presumed to be in a minority in any particular industry,
there can be little question of a specifically Catholic trade
union, although Catholics clearly have their work to do within
their trade union in order to prevent it from being captured
by materialistic and anti-religious forces. Pius also speaks of
the desirability of organizations among other than workers—
among, for instance, employers—commends them and regrets
that they are not stronger and more numerous. He reiterates
Leo's teaching about the rights of property, the desirability of
its wide distribution and the function of the State. Capital has
no right to offer to Labour only a bare subsistence wage.
Labour has no right to demand for itself the total value of the
product. Such generalizations, the critic may perhaps again
object, are platitudes, and, though the pope goes on to demand
a just distribution of wealth, he does not give any clear indica-
tion by what principle justice is to be assessed. Yet he clearly
shows the direction in which his mind is moving. The wage-
contract, argues Pius, is not inherently unjust. There is no
reason why one man should not hire another. But the relation
of employer-employee, he repeats from his predecessor, is not
an ideal relation. What is desirable is that every head of a family

should himself be the possessor of a little property and that
"the just wage" should be such that not only can the wage-
earner keep himself and his dependants in moderate comfort
but that he should also be able to save. Wherever possible an
enterprise should be an enterprise of partnership rather than
of employment. "We deem it advisable that the wage contract
should, when possible, be modified somewhat by a contract
of partnership." In calculating the just wage three things must
be considered.

It must be considered what is necessary to support the working man and his family. Catholic teaching cannot approve of
a system which, in order that the family may have a sufficiency,
compels the mothers and young children to go out to work.
Secondly, the state of the business must be considered. It is
idle to require a business to pay such wages that its costs of
production become uncompetitive, that it is unable to sell its
product. Thirdly, what the pope calls "the exigencies of the
common good" must be considered. By that he means princi-
pally that wages should be such as to maintain a general full
employment. There are two ways in which a mistaken wage-
policy can cause unemployment. If too high wages are paid
the product is unsaleable and the firm is driven into bank-
ruptcy with consequent unemployment. This was a familiar
enough point, which employers had with some relish been
making in answer to their employees' demands for higher
wages for more than a century. The pope's counter-point was
less familiar in 1931, though the experiences of the deflation of
the 1920's had given people plenty of opportunity to learn it.
It was that unemployment might equally be created by too low
a general level of wages. If too low wages were paid there was
an insufficiency of purchasing power to buy the nation's products. A sufficiency of purchasing power must be distributed
with a reasonable approach to equality because, though absolute mathematical equality was neither necessary nor desirable,
yet modern industrialism with its mass production threw on to
the market the sort of articles of which everybody wanted a
few and nobody wanted very many. Therefore, if incomes were
so distributed that a few had a great deal and the majority very

little, it must inevitably follow that goods which society produced would be unsaleable. In order to avoid this dilemma, Lenin had argued with a good deal of truth, colonial markets had been developed and investments made in them so that these colonial markets should be able to absorb the surplus products of Western imperialism. But it would obviously be both more equitable and less dangerous that those who produced the goods should be given sufficient purchasing power to buy them.

THE CORPORATIVE STATE

One of the great evils of the times, argued Pius, was the decay of subsidiary organizations. It is certainly true that in medieval Europe the individual had belonged to a number of subsidiary organizations—the guilds and such like—self-governing within their own limits. The years from the seventeenth century onwards had seen the steady decay of all such organizations. There was, for instance, little local government in nineteenth-century Britain. Such organizations as county councils were as yet unknown, and there were few intermediary authorities between the State on the one hand and the individual on the other. This, argued the pope, was unhealthy. Power should be diffused. There should be a profusion of subsidiary organizations, each possessed of its own authority within its proper sphere. The business of the State is not, with claims of omnicompetence, to seek to impose itself on all the details of the life of the citizen but rather as an arbitrator to prevent conflict between the various vocational groups. From that argument Pius came to sketch out his scheme of a corporative state. He considers the proposition that the form of self-government within a state should not be geographical but vocational.

The Church, it is said by Pius in this encyclical as it has also been said by its predecessors and by his successors, prescribes no ideal form of government. The citizens of a state must decide for themselves what form of government they prefer. Nevertheless the anti-clerical policy of the French Revolution had given many Catholics in the nineteenth century a bias against Parliamentarianism. Such Catholics welcomed the restoration of the *ancien régime* after 1815 and there was much talk among them of "an alliance between throne and altar". As a result, when after 1870 France adopted once more a republican form of government, some Catholics opposed it and thought it their duty to agitate for a return of the monarchy. Leo XIII rebuked them, told them that the republican form of government was not in itself incompatible with Catholicism and bade them accept the Republic and work within it. Pius XI in his day went so far as specifically to condemn the monarchist organ, the *Action Française*, not indeed, it is true, for being monarchist but because its free thinking editor, Charles Maurras, preached a doctrine of *politiques d'abord*, in which he advocated that the moral law should be subordinated to political convenience.

In Italy the story of Parliamentarianism was somewhat different from that of France. In Italy the Parliamentary régime was established in Rome in defiance of the pope's rights and Catholics were from the first forbidden to cooperate with it. When after a generation it became evident that Catholic abstention was not going to have the effect of destroying the Italian constitution but that it was merely going to make certain that there should be no Catholic influence on its policy the wisdom of it was doubtful and the policy was changed. Yet it can be seen that in Italy the Church had no especial bias, and had no cause to have any especial bias, in favour of the Parliamentary régime which had throughout all its history been alike corrupt, ineffective and anti-Catholic. Mussolini shortly after he came to power attempted to compose the quarrel of the Italian State with the Church by the Lateran Treaty. It is quite true that, no sooner were the Lateran Treaty and the accompanying Concordat signed, than the pope began to have grave anxieties about the Fascist Government's encroachments on education and uttered his protests. It would be out of place in such a work as this to attempt to tell, or to pass judgement on, the story in detail. *Quadragesimo Anno* was written in 1931. At that

time general world opinion about Mussolini was by no means
what it was to be in later years. Mussolini had begun his rule
indeed with a hooligan bombardment of the Greek island of
Corfu but after that many people had thought that he was
settling down into a sober Western statesman, anxious to
cooperate in the planning of peace. Hitler, Abyssinia, the German alliance—all lay in a distant and unforeseen future.
General opinion in the West in 1931 was not biased against
experiments because they were made by Mussolini, and Pius,
it must be admitted, was no exception to this rule.

Mussolini was proposing to substitute for the corrupt Parliament, based on territorial constituencies, a corporative
Chamber, in which representatives should be representatives
of the vocations. Pius was not unsympathetic to the idea. He
writes:

> Within recent times, as all are aware, a special syndical and
> corporative organization has been inaugurated which, in view of
> the subject of the present encyclical, demands of us some mention
> and opportune comment. The State here grants judicial per-
> sonality to the Union, and thereby confers on it some of the
> features of a monopoly; for, in virtue of this grant, it alone can
> uphold the rights of the workers or employers (according to the
> kind of Union) and it alone can negotiate wage-claims and make
> labour-agreements. Membership of the Union is optional, but
> only to this extent can the Union be said to be voluntary; because
> contributions to the Union and other special taxes are obligatory
> for all who belong to each trade or profession, whether workers
> or employers, and the labour agreements made by the legally
> established Unions are likewise binding on all. . . . The corpora-
> tions are composed of delegates of the Unions of workers and
> employers of the same trade or profession and, as true and genuine
> organs and institutions of the State, they direct and coordinate
> the activities of the Unions in all matters of common interest.

The pope comments: "Little reflection is required to per-
ceive the advantage of the situation thus summarily described,"
but even at this early date in Fascist history he noted that the
organs were not in practice the organs of a genuine industrial

self-government that they pretended to be. The State and the party had too much power. He wrote:

> We feel bound to say that to our knowledge there are those who fear that the State is substituting itself in the place of private initiative instead of limiting itself to necessary and sufficient assistance. It is feared that the new syndical and corporative organization tends to have an excessively bureaucratic and political character and that, notwithstanding the general advantages referred to above, it ends in serving particular political aims rather than in contributing to the initiation and promotion of a better social class.

The perversion of these new corporations into the instruments of Fascist policy, which the pope noted in the early days of the Fascist régime, became, as time went on, entirely inordinate until the régime became a wholly totalitarian and in no way a corporative régime. The Fascist régime proved itself to be anything but a Catholic régime, and the pope had at a later date in *Non Abbiamo Bisogno* to condemn not only this but many of its other features. The claim of the Italian Fascist régime to be a corporative régime of the kind advocated in *Quadragesimo Anno* showed itself to be wholly untenable. Such a régime was not found in Italy. Has it ever been found anywhere else? There are those who claimed that it was to be found in Dollfuss' Austria. But Dollfuss' Austria never had the basic unity which could make such an experiment genuine. Dollfuss was at war with the workers' organizations and turned the guns on them. Others have professed to find such an organization in Salazar's Portugal, but there again, though overt civil war has been avoided, no one can doubt that there are policies of repression and of the police state. We have yet to see an example of a country where the Government is held genuinely responsible not to a territorial but to a corporative Parliament. Corporative organizations, where they have been introduced, have in fact been but the façades for dictatorship.

In a further encyclical, *Divini Redemptoris* of 1937, Pius was to denounce Communism and to point to the evil effects of its propaganda throughout the world—in China, India, Spain and

Mexico—to denounce Catholic employers who had been in-different to the demands of *Rerum Novarum* and *Quadragesimo Anno*, and to reiterate the Catholic demand for a guild solution of economic problems. "The rôle of justice and charity," he wrote, "in social and economic relations can only be achieved when professional and interprofessional organizations, based on the solid foundations of Christian teaching, constitute, under forms adapted to different places and circumstances, what used to be called guilds." To further this, "It is of the utmost importance to foster in all classes of society an inten-sive programme of social education, adapted to the varying degrees of intellectual culture, and to spare no pains to procure the widest possible diffusion of social teaching of the Church among all classes, including the workers."

GERMANY AND ITALY

This is not the place to study in detail the complex story of the pope's relations with Fascist Italy and Nazi Germany. It is true that Pius XI was throughout his reign acutely conscious of the enormous danger of atheistic Communism. No one can deny that he was justified in this anxiety and it did certainly follow that, in so far as he thought of these régimes as enemies of Communism, he thought that it was to that extent a virtue in them. It led him to sign concordats with them, and it is likely that in the light of what happened later, a mistake was made in signing these concordats—in particular in signing that with Nazi Germany. But the signature of a concordat did not at all blind the pope to the fact that the policies of these régimes, even when they were opposed to an enemy of Catholic principles, were themselves the enemy of Catholic principles. In *Mit Brennender Sorge* and *Non Abbiamo Bisogno* he denounced the totalitarian claims of these régimes and in particular their ambition to bring under their own control all education and the entire youth of the country. But these quarrels, although of the greatest importance, were quarrels on political rather than on economic policy, and the details of them are therefore beyond the scope of this book.

In *Non Abbiamo Bisogno*, which had to be smuggled out of the Vatican and published in France, the pope denounced the Fascist régime's monopoly of youth "from the tenderest years up to manhood and womanhood, for the exclusive advantage of a régime based on an ideology which clearly amounts to a real pagan worship of the State—statolatry—which is no less in contradiction with the natural rights of the family than it is in contradiction with the supernatural rights of the Church". In the economic sphere he attacked the exclusion of Catholic Action from the corporations and syndicates which had replaced the trade unions. By that exclusion their true freedom as self-governing bodies was destroyed. The offences against Catholic and Christian doctrine of the Nazi régime in Germany were of course even more overt than those of the Fascist régime in Italy.

THE CHANGED ECONOMIC SITUATION SINCE LEO XIII'S TIME

More important are the pages in the encyclical in which the pope notes the changes in the economic system which have come in between 1891 and 1931. Leo XIII, like all the secular economists of the nineteenth century, when he spoke of the capitalist system, had in mind a system in which the factory was owned by one or by a few men and in which the workers worked for him for a wage. They thought of manager and owner as one and the same person. By 1931, as Pius notes, the structure had grown a great deal more complex, and it has grown even more complex since his day. Amalgamation and monopoly have created a new sort of capitalism. Immediately before 1914 all the important countries of the world lived under the monetary system of a gold standard, which few understood but which all took for granted. As a result of it the world had enjoyed a generally stable price level for ninety-nine years. The overwhelming majority thought that economic problems were to be solved within the framework of a monetary system which they had come to accept as both foolproof and automatic. With the outbreak of war in 1914 the gold standard

collapsed. Gold payments were suspended, and after the war
a deliberate decision had to be taken whether to return to the
gold standard or not.

The gold standard had behind it so great a prestige, the evils
of inflation in such countries as Germany, where currencies
had got completely out of control, were so apparent that
statesmen and bankers thought hardly any price too high to
pay for the psychological advantage of saying that their currencies were once again based on gold. But the truth is that
the world that emerged from the 1914 war was a very different
place from the world that went into it—in many respects, one
of which at least was highly relevant to monetary policies. In
the world before the war Great Britain was the great creditor
nation and Great Britain was also a free trade nation. The
nationals of other countries had their debts to pay to British
creditors and they could pay them by exporting whatever
goods they produced and selling them on the British market.
They could pay in goods, and as a result the mechanism of
international trade only required in exceptional cases the
transfer of gold from one country to another. The gold reserves
of every nation remained substantially stable and therefore
its monetary circulation remained substantially stable and
there were no violent fluctuations of the price level. But in
order to fight the 1914 war Great Britain had had to raise very
substantial loans and to underwrite the loans raised by her
continental allies in the United States. As a result the United
States which had previously been a debtor nation, borrowing
extensively in London and elsewhere for the building of its
great railways and for the general development of the country,
emerged from the war the greatest creditor nation in the world.
Now the United States as a creditor nation meant something
very different from Great Britain as a creditor nation. Great
Britain was poor in raw materials. For her industrial production she had to import almost all the raw materials except coal.
The United States in her much vaster area herself possessed
the greater number of the raw materials which industry
required. Rubber had indeed to be imported but most other

things were to be found in one place or another on the North American continent. Where Britain had been a free trade country, ready to accept payment in whatever goods a creditor might send along, the United States was a high tariff country, whose traditional policy it had been ever since the end of the Civil War to build up her own industries behind a tariff wall which protected them against foreign competition. After the war of 1914, so far from changing that traditional policy to conform to new circumstances, on the contrary with the Republican victory in the 1920 election she raised her tariff wall much higher by the so-called Fordney Tariff, so that it was impossible for any foreign article that competed with an American product to find its way on to the American market.

Yet Americans still demanded that foreigners pay their debts. The only commodity that was allowed free entry into the United States was gold. So they could only pay in gold and therefore it appeared inevitable that all the gold in the world would find its way across the Atlantic to the United States. Had the Americans been prepared to play the monetary game according to the pre-1914 rules, they must have thrown that gold on to the domestic market. The result would have been an American inflation of prices, resulting from an adherence to the gold standard, as catastrophic as the German inflation which resulted from the repudiation of the gold standard. Governor Benjamin Strong, then the Governor of the American Federal Reserve Bank, saw that such a rise in prices would create an unnecessary and undesirable disruption of American domestic life and therefore announced that the United States would make it the object of policy to maintain a stable domestic price level and that any gold holdings that were surplus to this requirement would not be given monetary effect but would be buried—"sterilized" as the phrase went. Looked at from the point of view of American interests, this was a sensible policy, but the result of it was of course that, since excessive gold holdings did not have their normal effect of raising American prices and thus making it more difficult for Americans to sell their goods abroad, in competition with lower-priced foreign

goods, there was no reason why any gold that found its way to
America should ever leave it again. Nor indeed did any gold
leave America in the 1920's except in so far as the Americans
made further deliberate loans and investments in Europe and
elsewhere. But these loans were no solution of the problem.
They merely postponed the day of reckoning. The Americans
demanded repayment of them, and there was no way in which
they could be repaid so long as the Americans refused to admit
foreign goods into their country.

It clearly followed that so long as gold was flowing to
America and there being sterilized, any other country must
have steadily decreasing gold holdings and, if it tied its currency to gold, must necessarily submit itself to a continuing
process of deflation with all the evil consequences of falling
prices and depression that necessarily go with deflation. It
was therefore great folly for any European Government—and
in particular the British Government—beguiled by the prestige
of the phrase "the gold standard" to choose such a time for
the basing of its currency on gold holdings. For they were
clearly not returning to the gold standard as it had existed
before 1914. They were rather establishing a system which by
the very rules of the gold standard could not work and which
was bound to lead to eventual collapse.

Yet the British Government declared the pound convertible
into gold in 1925. As a result during the second half of the
decade of the 'twenties both the British economy and that of
many continental countries were, to quote the phrase of Mr
Montague Norman, then the Governor of the Bank of England, "under the harrow". Deflation in Britain, which led to
unemployment in industry, led to a catastrophic fall in the
prices of foodstuffs on the London market. This in its turn
therefore led to a decline in American and Canadian farm incomes—since Britain was their main export market—to a con-
traction of their purchases—to a consequent disruption of the
American economy—to a panic American refusal to renew
overseas loans, which in its turn led to the collapse of the
economy of Central Europe, beginning with the Credit Anstalt

in Austria, and with that a general crisis which brought about
the formation of a National Government in Britain in 1931
and the general bank collapse in America, coincident with
Franklin Roosevelt's assumption of the Presidency in 1933.
At almost exactly the same time as Roosevelt came to power
in America Hitler came to power in Germany.

A MONETARY CRISIS

It is not the task of this book to analyse these events in
detail nor to seek to assess the enormous consequences that
flowed from them. The only point that it is necessary to make
is that here was a crisis that was entirely a crisis of money. The
world's productive capacity was greater than it had ever been.
Its political problems were not especially menacing—were
indeed in train of solution—and only became insoluble when
they were exacerbated by economic suffering. The world's collapse was entirely caused by the fact that those whose task it
was to manage its money had not performed their task with
sufficient skill.

This presented Pius XI with a challenge that was not in the
least present to Leo XIII's mind. In Leo's day most people—
and probably the pope himself among them—thought of the
management of money as a neutral, technical, almost automatic business that had little more bearing on the general
moral problems of the day than had the technical problems
of the construction of a steam-engine. Indeed Winston
Churchill, who was the British Chancellor of the Exchequer
at the time of the country's return to gold, was so ignorant of
the consequences of what he had done, that he said that the
resulting depression had no more to do with the gold standard
than it had to do with the Gulf Stream—an opinion which
Lord Keynes stigmatized as "feather-headed". Morality, Leo
had thought, was concerned with such questions as that of
property—what were the rights of property, what constituted
a proper title to property, how it should be distributed.
Direct attacks on property, whether by violence or by con-
fiscatory legislation, were condemned. It probably never

occurred to the pope that the property system could be much
more effectively destroyed by a monetary policy—by extravagant inflation or extravagant deflation—than it could be
either by legislation or by physical violence. Pius by his day
had learnt that lesson from experience, so some of the most
important passages in *Quadragesimo Anno* are those in which
he speaks of the masters of credit. These, he asserts, and not
the direct owners of property, are the real masters of a modern
State. Language about the class–war—about the conflict
between the "haves" and the "have-nots"—is not only un-
christian, it is also out of date. He speaks of the power of the
masters of credit in language which, considering the general
restraint of papal pronouncements, is extraordinarily and,
we may presume, designedly strong:

> In our days, not wealth alone is accumulated, but immense
> power and despotic economic domination are concentrated in the
> hands of a few, who for the most part are not the owners but only
> the trustees and directors of invested funds, which they administer
> at their own good pleasure. This domination is most powerfully
> exercised by those who, because they hold and control money,
> also govern credit and determine its allotment, for that reason
> supplying, so to speak, the life-blood to the entire economic
> body and, grasping in their hands, as it were, the very soul of
> production, so that no one dare breathe against their will. This
> accumulation of power is the characteristic note of the modern
> economic order.

It causes three separate types of relentless and evil struggle.
First there is the struggle for the mastery of the credit system.
Secondly, there is the struggle for the control of the State, and
thirdly, there is the struggle between the States.

Pius issued his encyclical, as we have said, in March 1931.
It was in the autumn of that year that the British Labour
Government resigned in favour of a National Government
and shortly afterwards the gold standard in Britain was suspended. The result of the suspension of the gold standard was
that throughout the 1930's, and subsequently, both Britain
and other countries had a managed currency. The monetary

supply has been dependent not on the accident of gold holdings but on deliberate Treasury policy. The object of policy
throughout the 1930's was to maintain a stable price level and
up till the outbreak of war that object was, broadly, achieved.
The necessities of war and of a rapid rebuilding of the economy
in the years after the war involved measures of inflation, and
it was not until 1958 that, through a combination of circumstances and Government policy, it was possible to hold prices
stable for any considerable period of time. This is not the
place to consider the details of these policies nor to argue
whether or not matters could have been better managed. The
only point which it is important to make is that by an accident
a few months after the pope had made his protest against a
system in which monetary supply was so completely under the
control of financiers, the system collapsed and since then
monetary supply has been a matter for conscious Government
regulation, wise or unwise, and the financiers have been much
less powerful. Whereas in the 1920's the troubles of the
economy came from deflation, since the last war they have come
from inflation. The consequence of this has been that of the
three struggles, of which the pope spoke, the struggle between
the financiers has been much less intense than heretofore,
whereas the struggle to get control of the State has been more
intense. Of the struggles between States there is, alas, no need
to remind the reader. These struggles were by no means wholly
economic struggles, but economics played their large part in
embittering them.

The struggle for the mastery of the State had already produced, when the pope wrote, and most certainly has since produced, what he calls "crying evils" arising from "the inter-
mingling and scandalous confusion of the functions and duties
of civil authority and of the economic organization". "The
State which should be the supreme arbiter, ruling in kingly
fashion far above all party contention, intent only upon justice
and the common good, has become instead a slave, bound over
to the service of human passion and greed." Two evils have
shown themselves, "economic nationalism or even economic

imperialism" and "a detestable internationalism," which leads men, in indifference to all other ties, to be concerned only to discover in what part of the world they can make the most money. That is to say, Pius seems to speak as if there had been at some time some sort of "natural" order of society in which productive activity was entirely the business of private individuals, and the only concern of the State was with impartial justice to enforce contracts and to prevent men from cheating one another. When a society of such a sort existed, however much liberal economists may have argued that it ought to exist, is by no means clear, but certainly Pius rendered an important service in reminding us that society was constantly developing and that text-book descriptions of its economic organization that may have been true in the nineteenth century and in the days of Leo were no longer necessarily true a generation later. It is a reminder that is needed again today.

THE CHURCH AND SOCIALISM

The pope then comes on to consider the suggested remedies for society's problems. Leo had spoken of Socialism and had condemned it. In his day there was no socialistic society in existence and he considered Socialism simply as a theory which denied that there was any right of property. By Pius' time in talking of Socialism it was necessary to consider not merely theories but also facts. Pius distinguishes. There are different kinds of Socialism. First, there is Communism—the form of government that had been established by violence in Russia. This preaches open class war, denies the right of property and is confessedly atheist. The pope condemned it without qualification. But there is a more moderate Socialism, which seeks to obtain power by constitutional means. When Leo wrote, no constitutional Socialist had established himself in power in any European country. By the time that Pius wrote there had been a number of examples of Socialist ministers and Socialist governments. A Socialist Government was in office in Britain at the time of the publication of the encyclical.

What is the attitude of the Church towards Socialism of such a sort ?

It is a practical question of some importance, and also of some difficulty. It is never altogether easy to define the attitude of the Church towards various other philosophies of life— economic and political doctrines and the like—because, whereas the Church's doctrine is hard, definite and unchanging, these other "isms", as it is often the fashion to call them, accept no defining authority. Men use the word in different senses at different times and in different places. Whatever the teaching of the Church towards Socialism, it is, for instance, quite certain that a Catholic is not in any way forbidden to belong, or indeed discouraged from belonging, to such a body as the British Labour party. Such parties are often called Socialist parties. Their members often call themselves Socialists. It might seem a somewhat profitless verbalism to say that they are not really Socialists, when they call themselves such, since there is obviously no authoritative copyright in the word and it would, we might say, have been a little more helpful if the popes had used another word to signify what they were condemning.

The fact clearly is that those who formed the Socialist parties in Leo's time did not even pretend to be other than anti-religious, and therefore Catholic sociology formed, and has continued, the habit of using the word in Leo's sense, even though others have come to use it in a somewhat different sense and there are today those who call themselves Socialists and are at the same time good Catholics and they incur no ecclesiastical censure. What has the pope to say about these constitutional Socialists ? There are, he argues, two kinds of Socialists of this sort. There are those who, though they do not preach violent revolution, yet demand the total abolition of property and nationalization of all the means of production and distribution. These, though less blameworthy than the full Communists, are nevertheless to be condemned. No Catholic can hold such doctrines. But there are on the other hand those who, though they call themselves Socialists, nevertheless not only eschew violence and the class war but also admit—at any rate to some extent—the right of property. Of this Socialism the pope writes:

> Not only does it condemn recourse to violence; it even miti-
> gates class warfare and the abolition of private property and
> qualifies them to some extent, if it does not actually reject them.
> ... It would seem as if socialism were afraid of its own prin-
> ciples and the conclusion drawn therefrom by Communists, and
> in consequence were tending towards the truths which Christian
> tradition has always held in respect for it cannot be denied that
> its opinions sometimes closely approach the just demands of
> Christian social reformers. [In such people's mouths] it is not the
> possession of the means of production which is attacked but a
> form of social authority which property has usurped in violation
> of all justice.   [Pius XI foresees the possibility that] these tenets
> of mitigated socialism will no longer be different from the pro-
> gramme of those who seek to reform human society according
> to Christian principles [and he agrees that] certain forms of pro-
> perty must be reserved to the State, since they carry with them a
> power too great to be left to private individuals without injury to
> the community at large.

He only asks why such people should wish to call themselves Socialists. The reason why they wish to call themselves Socialists is in truth not obscure. It is not an easy thing to found a new political party, and those who wish to exercise influence must usually work through an existing party and to do so must to some extent use the language which is habitual to it. In the world of theory people think of a programme and form a party to implement it. In the world of practice people take an existing party and attempt to convert it to their pro-gramme. The pope doubtless understood this well enough. All that he demanded of such reformers was that they in no way mitigate their Christian principles in a vain hope of going half way to meet the dogmatic Socialists. "Whether considered as a doctrine, or as an historical fact, or as a movement, Social-ism, if it really remains socialism," he ruled "cannot be brought into harmony with the dogmas of the Catholic

Church." It would, perhaps, have been simpler if he had avoided the word "Socialism" and said instead, "The Catholic Church cannot deny a right of property".

The general pattern of what seems to be happening more or less over the whole world during the quarter of a century or more since Pius wrote his encyclical is this. On the one hand it has been proved that enthusiasm for nationalization is limited. Certain acts of nationalization have been carried through in all countries, but equally in all countries even the most extreme Socialists no longer have any wish to carry through a complete abolition of all private property. On the other hand, the very fact that the private financier has been brought under some measure of control has increased the importance for the politician of making himself master of the State which controls them. In all States today, both in those which call themselves Socialist and those which call themselves Conservative and capitalist, the State has much more control over both credit and industry than would have been thought reasonable a generation ago and modern technological developments require such large units of production that there are inevitably many more forms of property which, to quote the pope's words, carry with them a power too great to be left to private individuals than there used to be. In such a world it is difficult to see how we can give as large a place to individual private property as we should like to give, but it is arguable that it is increasingly circumstances rather than the ideological preferences of the politicians which dictate the economic pattern of States and that those States which call themselves Socialist and those which call themselves anti-Socialist are in fact daily becoming steadily more like to one another.

Why does Catholicism insist so strongly on the rights of property? There are those who argue that a system of private property is more efficient than a system of State socialism—that we are likely to get greater productivity if the incentives of sticks and carrots are recognized. This may well be true—or at least true in more instances than not—and, if so, the economist and the politician are right to insist on it. But such truths are clearly no part of revealed religious truth. The reason why the Catholic, as such, must be opposed to extreme Socialism is not primarily an objection to a particular economic system so much as an objection to the assertion that economic prosperity is the sole concern of society. As we have seen, early Fathers, such as St Chrysostom and St Ambrose, by no means shared this concern of the latter day Church for the preservation of the property system. They condemned property as a cause of selfishness. It was not possible for them to see a property system as a bulwark against a too powerful State. The Catholic objects to the extreme Socialist because he is only concerned to obtain as high a material standard of living as possible, and by the same token, if the anti-socialist demonstrates that Socialism is not the most efficient system but that he objects to it only on those grounds, the Catholic must equally take issue with him. So the pope makes clear that his fundamental quarrel with Socialism is not in so far as it is an economic doctrine but in so far as it is a cultural doctrine. He objects to the "cultural Socialism" which subordinates all man's activities to the sole service of the State—in fact to what a little later came to be fashionably called totalitarianism.

Pius XII in his radio message of 1944 made it clear that the Church advocated ownership not merely for its economic advantages but "for the benefit of the freedom and dignity of Man created in the image of God," and in fact during the rest of Pius XI's life his main quarrels were to be with States which made totalitarian claims, while professing opposition to Communism—with States which repudiated the Socialist theory in economics (even though, it is true, it was not always very easy to see exactly how they repudiated the socialist practice), with Nazi Germany, which he denounced in *Mit Brennender Sorge*, and with Fascist Italy, which he denounced in *Non Abbiamo Bisogno*.

The story of the relations of the Vatican with Germany and Italy throughout the nineteen thirties is a complicated one. Admittedly there was not so overt a breach as many Liberals would have liked. We are here only concerned with the Church's economic doctrine. The pope's final conclusions are concerned with morality. The Church's concern is with the salvation of souls. No economic system which seeks to make either prosperity or power more important than virtue can be a Christian economic system. By that test there is no difficulty in saying that the economic system of Germany and Italy, and of course Russia, in the inter-war years must be condemned. The more difficult question is how far the economic system of any other countries in those years, or indeed in these years, is to be commended. An economic system which bases itself uncompromisingly on the text *Radix malorum est cupiditas* is a sufficiently overt challenge to most of the economic systems of the day. If it is difficult to extract from it exact guidance which political party to support, the reason surely is that it is difficult to find in any country a political party that lives up to it.

But how far, the critic may ask, does the pope's encyclical help us to answer such a question? What on the last analysis does he tell us? He condemns the irresponsible rich, but at the same time he puts his veto on the very policies—nationalization and penal taxation—by which alone, many people would argue, can the rich be effectively attacked. They are, it seems, to be brought to a sense of responsibility by little except by the promptings of their own consciences. What hope is there that such promptings would be effective? On the other hand the pope attacks Socialism, but then at once qualifies his attack by saying that it is only directed against those who are "properly called" Socialists and not against all who call themselves Socialists. Had the encyclical forbidden any Catholic to give his support to any party that called itself Socialist, then, whether the encyclical was right or wrong, we could not complain that it was not giving clear guidance. As it is, it is hard to know with certainty at whom it is hitting. It is true that the encyclical shows some general sympathy with distributist policies—with those who, rather than concentrate all property into the hands of a few men or into the hands of the State—would like to see it widely distributed so that, as

nearly as possible, every head of a family has his small property, and the Church, we gather, has a natural sympathy with
such policies as co-partnership and profit-sharing. But how
this policy of the distribution of property is to be applied to
an industrial society, where the unit of production must so
often be a very large unit, the encyclical does not clearly say,
nor does it tell us whether it is desirable that the working man's
little nest-egg of property should be in a few shares in the
industry in which he works—thus making him a co-partner—
or in some other industry so as to give him relief in a day of
calamity if his own industry should fall upon hard times. The
two views depend upon two quite separate conceptions of the
function of property.

Supposing that we were considering the pope as a party
political leader sketching out a party programme, these criticisms would have great force. But, as has already been said,
the pope is not the leader of a political party nor is the Church
a political party. In the economic sphere the Church does not
profess for the most part to tell us what answers to give. It is
concerned to tell us what questions to ask. Schemes of profit
sharing will work easily in some industries—in those generally
in which profits are constant—and are much harder to apply
in others. It is not the business of the pope to give us a list of
the industries to which such schemes are suited and to propose
to us alternative schemes for the industries to which they are
not suited. It is his task to bid us discover the answers to such
questions for ourselves and to warn us that we neglect such a
command at our peril—not only at peril of economic disloca-
tion but at peril to our immortal souls. The final conclusion
of the encyclical is that all these technical problems can only
be solved if there is first a moral reformation within men's
souls which causes them to turn away from selfishness and
greed. Without such a reformation no economic system, however technically perfect, can hope to succeed. And if the critic,
turned cynic, asks what hope there is of such a reformation,
it is of course the Church's answer that she has never held
out any prospects of an easy Utopia. Man, she well knows, is

born in sin and she does not expect too much of him. On the other hand, if we are forbidden presumption, we are equally forbidden despair. "These are they for whom their Omnipotent Creator did not disdain to die."

CATHOLIC POLITICAL PARTIES

Yet there is a more particular criticism which can be urged against modern Catholic economic policies and which it is only right honestly to face. It is all very well, the critic may say, to talk about these phases of society—to say that in the Middle Ages the accident of circumstances had brought into being a Catholic society and that in such a state it was natural that the Church should give rulings—that today the Church is spread out across the world in a way unparalleled in previous history —that the majority of Catholics today live in societies in which the majority of their fellow citizens are not Catholic—that this is an age for the enunciation of moral principle—where possible of moral principle which Catholic and non-Catholic can unite in accepting—rather than for mandatory ruling. That is what you say when you are talking in non-Catholic countries, anxious to show non-Catholics how reasonable and liberal you are. But what happens in Catholic countries or in countries which we are able to call Catholic countries? Italy, for instance, is a Catholic country in the sense that of those who profess a religion at all the overwhelming majority profess the Catholic religion and in such a country the Church is by no means willing to follow a policy of neutrality between political parties. She does not content herself with forbidding the faithful to support the Communists, or even with forbidding them to support any politicians who are prepared to act with the Communists. None of these distinctions, between "Socialists properly so-called" and those who call themselves Socialists but to a large extent proclaim Catholic principles, which the pope was so careful to draw in his encyclical, appear to be much considered in practice. If the faithful are not absolutely commanded under pain of mortal sin to vote for Christian Democratic candidates, at least there is many a sermon from the

pulpit the tenor of which is that a Catholic would be a very
peculiar and suspect Catholic should he dream of doing anything else. It is true that when Signor de Gasperi was the leader
of the Christian Democratic party he was careful to insist that
his party, even when it held a clear majority of seats, should
only undertake government in coalition with other parties so
that no one should have the excuse of saying that this was a
Catholic Government. But he was attacked in some clerical
circles for doing so. It is true, too, that recent electoral results,
whether in the North of Italy in Aosta or in the South in
Sicily, would seem to show that many who consider themselves
good Catholics do not in fact follow the guidance which the
priests offer to them. But, if the intransigence of the clergy is
in fact to some extent mitigated by the disobedience of the
laity, no one can pretend that that is a satisfactory solution.
Similarly, while it may well be a sign of wisdom that the
Christian Democrats should after the election enter into coalition with other parties, in some ways that makes it only the
more puzzling if Catholics are discouraged from voting for
candidates of those parties at the election.

Yet the Catholic Church is a free society, and there is no
pretence that the possession of faith carries with it protection
against detailed errors in tactics. There is a case for, and a case
against, Catholic political parties and whether such a party
is on balance desirable depends on the particular circumstances
of each particular case. One of the main disadvantages to be
set off against its advantages is that such a party, like all
political parties, is sure to make its mistakes and that then
there is an inevitable danger that the Church will suffer for
those mistakes.

We have the phenomenon of what is loosely called a
Catholic political party in many other countries besides Italy.
In France there is no pretence that every Catholic is under
obligation to support, or does support, the M.R.P. In Germany many Protestants join with Catholics in supporting the
Christian Democrats and, if few Catholics—or indeed few
professing Christians—are found among the Social Democrats,

that is not so much because of Christian intransigence as because the Social Democrats have until recently seen fit to present themselves as a specifically non-Christian party. There are signs that they are now breaking with that tradition, and, if they do so completely, it is likely that in Germany politics will present a less confessional appearance and those Catholics who favour a different economic policy from that of the ruling powers of the Christian Democrats will find other parties for the advocacy of them. In Holland there is a tradition of confessional parties—alike among Protestants as among Catholics —but there again the Catholics, standing separately at the elections, have cooperated after' elections with other parties in coalition governments, sometimes with the Protestants and sometimes with the Socialists.

It is not the task of this book to foretell future political developments—still less, to estimate the pace at which they will take place. Doubtless there will always be particular questions upon which it is desirable that Catholics stand together, but it would seem inevitable, whatever the ecclesiastical authorities may desire, that political parties will bear a steadily decreasing confessional stamp. It is with no disrespect for ecclesiastical authorities that one writes thus but simply because it appears inevitable. In the simpler economy of the past, the economy of self-contained units, it was possible —whether it was desirable or not—to have a Protestant village, a Catholic village in the next valley—if you will, a free thinking or a Mohammedan village beyond it. Our economy is not of that sort. We are now throughout the whole of society dependent on one another's goods and services to an extent of which our ancestors would never have dreamed. Our economy, whatever its pattern, must inevitably be of one kind. We cannot have a Catholic railway system and a Protestant railway system and a secularist railway system. We can only have a railway system. Therefore the Church, if she is to exercise economic influence, can only exercise it by enunciating teaching that is generally accepted by society, Catholic and non-Catholic. Warnings addressed merely to the Catholics are important in preventing individuals from sin, but, in so far as they are to effect policies, they must be heeded both by Catholic and non-Catholic. Therefore, since politics are to so large an extent dominated by economics, it will become increasingly desirable that Catholics and non-Catholics should work together in political parties.

It is reasonable to hope that such cooperation will bring to the non-Catholics a better understanding of, and a greater sympathy for, the Catholic position and will save Catholics from the horrible temptation of questioning the good faith of their fellow Catholics who differ from them in political opinions upon which there is no dogmatic teaching of the Church. The anti-clericalism of such continental parties as the Belgian Socialist party has been to a considerable extent an almost inevitable reaction from the challenge of a Catholic political party, for which all Catholics were expected to vote and which sought to put in office a Government that was exclusively Catholic. With a decline of confessional parties it is reasonable to expect a decline of anti-clericalism.

THE CHURCH AND INTERNATIONAL SOCIAL JUSTICE

There arises out of that a far deeper criticism than any that has yet been made by our imagined critic of papal social policies. Pius, as we have seen, noted certain developments of society that had taken place since Leo. Further developments again have taken place since Pius or were taking place in his day. The age of the Catholic society is passing. Catholics, who had played so small a part in European Parliamentary life in the previous generations, were able for the first time to obtain predominant positions in the Parliaments of almost all of the European nations in post-war days. Schumann and after him de Gaulle in France, de Gasperi in Italy, Adenauer in Germany —between them their power was such that unfriendly critics denounced the Council of Europe or projects for European Federation or the Common Market as Vatican plots. Yet the more perceptive were well aware that by a curious irony Europe was becoming more Catholic at the very moment that it was becoming less powerful. Perhaps it was becoming more Catholic because it was becoming less powerful, for power certainly corrupts and humiliation purges. In any case, the fact is that the typical Catholic no longer lives in a purely Catholic society and—what is more important—incomparably the greater part of the most vigorous Catholic thinking today comes from Catholics who are citizens of mixed countries where only a minority practise the Catholic religion. On the other hand, the spread of industrialism throughout the world has had the incidental consequence that Catholics today are far more widely scattered than they have been in any past age. There is no country in the world which has not today its Catholic communities both native and foreign, and there is no doubt that, as travel becomes easier and more rapid, Catholics will be yet more widely distributed.

The consequence has been a profound change in the accidents of Catholic life. In the early years of this century Belloc could write without self-evident absurdity in his *Europe and the Faith*: "Europe is the Faith, and the Faith is Europe." Overwhelmingly the greater number and overwhelmingly the most important proportion of Catholics were either residents of Western Europe or at least of Western European origin, and in America the Catholics of the United States were still so poor that in the early years of this century collections were taken in European churches for their support. The entire government of the Church could be concentrated in European hands without apparent injustice and without raising protest. Pius XII fully understood that that era had passed—that the Church was now a world-wide body in fact as well as in theory and no longer merely a European organization. In his Christmas message of 1945 he said:

> In former times the life of the Church, in its visible aspect, deployed its strength preferably in the countries of Europe from which it spread out like a majestic river to what may be called the periphery of the world. Today on the contrary it is manifested as an exchange of life and energy between all the members of Christ's Mystical Body on earth. Many countries in other continents have long since passed beyond the missionary stage in their ecclesiastical organizations; they are governed by their own hierarchy and they contribute spiritually and materially to the whole Church, whereas formerly they did nothing but receive.

He appointed to the Sacred College cardinals from India,

Syria, Armenia and China. His successor has added cardinals from Japan, the Philippines, Mexico and Tanganyika. The effect of this world-wide extension of Catholicism on the Church's economic teaching has still to be faced.

In the past effective economic units have always been of limited area. The economic problems have been how incomes and property should be distributed, how production should be organized, within a limited area. One area has indeed exchanged its products with another area in trade, and the volume of trade has over the generations been steadily on the increase. Nevertheless each area—in recent times each nation—has been considered responsible for its own social problems and considered not to have responsibility for the problems of another nation. We in England or America, for instance, stated that Italy was a poor country. We were merely stating a fact. We were beginning to feel, however, imperfectly, that we had some responsibility for the poor of our own nation, but it never occurred to us that we had any duty to do anything to relieve the general poverty of Italy. We read in the papers of a flood or a famine in China. Very occasionally we might subscribe for the relief of its victims. Most often we would not do even that. Very rarely did it occur to us that we had any responsibility to remedy the conditions that brought about that catastrophe.

Today the whole moral climate is different. For better or worse the whole world is becoming—has indeed to a large extent already become—a single economic unit. The motives which have brought about this unification have been largely materialistic and secular, but, whether good or bad, the unification is a fact that we cannot escape. Today it is becoming almost a platitude that the first object of policy must be to raise the standards of the under-developed nations. Recognizing this duty, we often ease our consciences in a not very attractive fashion by sanctimonious confession of the sins of our grandparents. We blame them because, as we allege, so little was done to develop colonial territories in the past. I am not at all sure how far that blame is deserved. The British are blamed for not developing India. As George Orwell has pointed out, one has only to compare a map of the railway system of British India with that of neighbouring countries that remained independent to see that Britain did a great deal more towards developing India than any of those other countries ever did towards developing themselves. Nor, in so far as the British did not do more, is it by any means clear how far it was their fault. Thirty-odd years ago I remember listening to a speech made by Mr Gandhi in Calcutta in which he denounced Western investment in India on the ground that the industrial development of the country would inevitably destroy the Indian way of life. Nor indeed, when we talk today about our duty to help the under-developed countries, is it certain how far our motive is one of genuine good will and how far we are merely concerned to prevent them from falling to the Communists.

Still, whatever the mixture of motives that are bringing it into existence, the fact that this new world is coming into existence is certain and, coming into existence, it raises all sorts of questions on which it is urgently necessary that we know the mind of the Church. At present there are vast differences between the standards of living in the different countries and between continent and continent. Is this disparity just? If it be just, what is the criterion by which such differences should be settled? The most doctrinaire of egalitarians would not demand that all incomes all over the world should suddenly be equalized tomorrow. But, as things are, there seems every reason to think that, far from moving towards equality, the gap between the standards in the rich nations and the standards in the poor nations is widening. Is this tolerable? If not, how can it be remedied? The two encyclicals were written on the assumption that the economic unit was the nation. They discussed what should be the organization of industry and the distribution of income within the nation. Their references to international conditions were passing and ephemeral. The result is that on the great moral problems created by the new internationalism the Church has up till now given little guidance. The Communists are ready enough with their reckless promises and the sceptic may very well ask how many of these promises would be fulfilled, what sort of equality there would be for the formerly subject peoples if the Communists should ever come to power. But it must be confessed that the Church up till the present has not given very much in the way of a positive answer on the principles on which in Catholic eyes this new international order should be built. She discusses what are the conditions of a just war, in what circumstances nations may properly fight one another. She has up to the present had less to say on what are the conditions of a just peace. Doubtless, when the time is ripe, the pope will give a more detailed exposition of the Church's teaching on these new problems.

Yet, though many problems still remain to be solved and many answers to be expounded, the outline of the Catholic teaching arises inevitably out of the very nature of the faith. The Christian religion describes our social obligations under the title of "our duty towards our neighbour", and that phrase clearly implies the truth that, as a general rule, men will find their opportunities to serve their fellows in service to those who live near to them. But our Lord from the first made it clear that we cannot invoke the word "neighbour" as a justification of indifferences towards anyone just because he does not happen to be of our locality. We cannot in effect have much obligation to those with whom we cannot communicate. But once, for whatever reason, good or bad, secular or religious, our culture has become interlocked with another culture, that interlocking imposes upon us obligations. In the Middle Ages Christendom, in relation to the non-Christian world, had been a city under siege, defending itself against the Moslem who threatened to overrun it. With the discovery of America the Christian world for the first time found itself able to expand and consequently faced with the moral problems which such a possibility created.

Sepulveda, chaplain to Charles V, greeted the discovery as a gift from God. Christians, he thought, had a full right to take possession of these non-Christian lands. The pre-conquest Indians had no right to the property of which they were found in possession. Both Catholics and Protestants—but Protestants more than Catholics—were guilty of re-introducing into Christendom the evil institution of slavery which the Church had stamped out a thousand years before and the yet greater evil of the slave-trade.

Yet from the first there was a Catholic tradition which vigorously repudiated the notion that the Catholic had a right to use his discoveries for mere purposes of exploitation. The great Dominican thinker Vittoria[1] vigorously disputed this thesis. The papal line dividing the possessions in the new world between Spain and Portugal could only have the effect, he argued, of placing a boundary so as to prevent conflict between Spain and Portugal. The right of personal property in America, belonged to the Indian inhabitants. The pope had no power to deprive them of that right. They did not forfeit it by not being Christians. The only right of a Christian colonist was a right to trade freely with the natives. Suarez,[2] the Jesuit theologian, agreed with him. Las Casas, in his attempts to impose a humane code of conduct on his fellow Spaniards, followed Vittoria's teaching.

It is of course true that, whatever the Church might teach, there was no effective force to prevent a well-armed colonist, avid for wealth, from ill-treating an ill-armed native, and shameful things were done in Spanish and Portuguese colonies. The Catholic record, for what it is worth, is better than the Protestant. Catholics did not exterminate their aborigines as Protestants in North America and Australia so often did. H. A. L. Fisher, a Protestant historian, has written,

> The Roman Church honourably endeavoured to improve the lot of the labouring population in the Spanish colonies. The slave was baptised, prepared for the Mass, retained in his family group and brought through his membership of the Church within the system of Spain. For the British colonies the Church of England made no comparable effort. While the Spanish Church pushed forward on its missionary enterprise the British planters looked

[1] 1480–1546.
[2] 1548–1617.

with active disfavour on the attempt to spread among the blacks the disturbing ferment of Christian belief.[3]

Grotius, in the next century, when he expounded his doctrine of the Law of Nations, insisted on an absolute right of trade. The possessor of property, argued Grotius, must not be deprived of his property, but the right to trade was absolute. "Not even temporal sovereigns in their own dominions have the right to prohibit freedom of trade," he wrote.[4]

The trouble with such theories, greatly as they are to be praised for their enlightened liberality, is that they give no guidance on one of the problems where guidance is most clearly called for. There is a more complex problem than that of man's mere greed and wickedness. Suppose that there are two societies of a reasonable equality of development. It is easy and right to say that neither should attempt to seize the other's property by force and that they should rather trade freely together to their mutual advantage. But suppose, as was in fact the case in both the Americas and in more recent times in Australia, the newly discovered land is inhabited indeed but grossly under-populated. Its natives have neither the numbers nor the skill to produce from it the wealth that it is capable of producing. There is a private right of property. There is a general right of use. There must come a point where, if he neglects to use his property, the possessor of it forfeits his right to it. Where is that point? What degree of pressure is the colonizing power justified in using to make the natives more efficient? At what point, if any, is it justified in stepping in to take possession of all, or a part, of the new land so as to ensure that it produces more nearly to its capacity? Of course particular acts of cruelty or treachery against aborigines are to be condemned. That is evident, but such condemnations do not meet the real point, Is the seizure of the aborigines' country justified, and, if so, under what circumstances?

It was because they did not answer these problems that the theories of Vittoria and Grotius were in practice comparatively

[3] *History of Europe*, Vol. III, p. 1029.
[4] *Grotius*, By W. S. M. Knight, p. 105.

ineffective. Tough colonists solved with brutality the problem of the treatment of natives which the philosophers and the theologians had told them how to solve with humanity. By the nineteenth century we had the era of imperialism. All Africa except Abyssinia and all Asia except Japan was by the end of that century either the direct possession, or within the sphere of influence of one or other of the European Powers. The imperial masters developed the resources of their colonies. It is true that they drew wealth out of them for themselves, but at the same time they left more wealth behind in the subject lands than they had enjoyed before these European masters came. There was an increased population to clamour for its share of that increased wealth. Irrigation schemes, famine relief, better communications were introduced. Order was maintained and justice was administered incomparably better than it had been in pre-imperial days. Where the balance lay between the good and the bad of such a system it is not easy to say. It is not possible to pass on it sweeping condemnation or sweeping approval.

What is certain is that there was little attempt to face the question whether there was a moral obligation to raise Oriental wages so as to bring them more nearly into line with Western wages—whether, to use the Catholic terminology, the just wage east of Suez was something quite different from the just wage west of Suez. People rather contented themselves by merely stating as a fact that Oriental labour was "cheap" and, if challenged for a justification, would add that it was "inefficient". How far it is in fact inherently inefficient, how far it is in general true that the Oriental, taught how to use a tool or work a machine, does so less efficiently than the white worker wise men would today feel less certain than their grandparents. It is true that, up to the present, experience seems to show that the Oriental can work a machine but he has not yet proved himself very competent at inventing one, but no one can say that he will not soon begin even to invent. Anyway, the important truth about the phase of imperialism is not so much that it was good or bad as that it was ephemeral. It was inevitable that sooner or later the Oriental, having been taught how to use a machine, would insist in using it for his own advantage rather than for that of the white man. The imperialistic system in Asia collapsed utterly—perhaps more suddenly than was desirable—with the second World War. It is clear that the imperialistic system in Africa will not endure very much longer.

Yet of course it is by no means true that the European masters have gone, leaving Oriental society to resume the pattern that it had before they came. On the contrary, the old rulers such as they were—the Sultans and the Rajahs—have gone out in the European baggage train. Sweeping generalizations are unsatisfactory, but on the whole its traditional religions with the sole exception of Islam show little sign of either retaining or regaining their hold on the Oriental mind. Buddhism seems to survive more as a nationalist political than as a religious creed. The Orient is left to a spiritual vacuum— to an empty worship of the materialistic techniques of the West. The West's tradition of political freedom they have proved in general unable to absorb and the pattern of Oriental government seems to be one of a military dictatorship, which, were the word not so out of fashion, it would be most convenient to call Fascism.

In the secular sphere there has been some, if insufficient, recognition of the new patterns. When at the end of the 1914 war, the Western Powers accepted the principle of self-determination, it was generally assumed that that principle did not apply to colonial territories. Yet the League of Nations did give a certain recognition to the economic problems of such countries in the International Labour Organization. With this war our recognition of such problems became more explicit. Roosevelt and Churchill in the Atlantic Charter, signed on August 14th, 1941, pledged themselves to give to all nations the right to trade and free access to raw materials. The United Nations Charter has established a variety of specialized agencies, the World Health Organization, UNESCO, the Food and Agricultural Organization, etc., to consider world economic and world cultural problems. If the world is an economic unity, then it perhaps logically follows that there should be a World Government and a World Authority. It may be that we are moving towards such a Government and that without it we cannot hope for a full solution of our problems. One day perhaps we shall see the old dualism of Pope and Emperor—not of course necessarily with monarchical secular authority—recreated on a truly world scale. That, if at all, is for a distant future. All that we can say is that there are today many more secular organizations which are at least giving their minds to world economic problems and to the world as an economic unity than ever before.

Yet, though technical research is necessary, technical research cannot in itself bring us to a solution of our problems until we have first settled the principles by which they should be solved. What is the relationship between European and Oriental living standards which justice requires? The question has not up to the present been clearly answered whether by the Church or by any other competent authority. The Right to Life has, it is true, been affirmed, but there has been no clear definition what exactly it means. Does it mean that there is a duty to pay such a wage that the Oriental worker and his family do not actually starve? We must all agree that it means more than that. Does it mean that we ought to pay him such a wage that the Oriental expectation of life is equal to the European? It would require a gigantic revolution to bring that about in every country of Asia and Africa and, if we were to insist on doing it suddenly, we could only do it by reducing the European standard. Does justice require that we take such measures? To what extent are we under obligation to distribute the luxuries of life equally among the different races of the world? What degree of inequality is tolerable? How far is our duty towards our neighbour not merely a duty towards the living but also a duty towards those who are to come— towards posterity? At what point does it become a sin recklessly to squander natural resources at the expense of posterity —even though they be equally distributed among the living?

Or migration? With the decrease of infant mortality owing to improved conditions and improved medicine—obviously in themselves good things—there was a vast increase in the world's white population in the nineteenth century. The population of Europe multiplied by about four, but there were perhaps eight times as many people of European origin in the world in 1900 as there had been in 1800. The surplus had found homes because they had been able to emigrate to the new white-inhabited countries outside Europe. Since the 1914 war there have been much more severe restrictions on immigration and the restrictions have undoubtedly been one of the great causes of world tension. What is the Catholic teaching on the right of migration? Has a man a natural right to go to whatever country he wishes just as Grotius thought that he had a natural right to trade freely? Under what circumstances has the receiving country a right to refuse him? Has it such a right if its only motive is to maintain for itself a higher standard of living than that of the generality of mankind? Have we a duty to welcome racial mixture, or a right to take measures to prevent it?

There is an immediate obligation on the wealthy countries to make the capital investments in the under-developed countries so as to enable them to industrialize themselves. (But there is much less reason than used to be thought to believe that there is an inherent difference in efficiency between the labour of one nationality and another.) Differences in productivity are due much more to differences in capital equipment than to differences in the individual worker's efficiency. Therefore, there is little reason to think that, when they are capitally equipped the Oriental countries will not produce as much per worker as the Occidental and, when that happens, there will be no reason in justice why their wages should not be similar. Pius XII in his 1952 Christmas Broadcast condemned the notion that the people of one nation had any natural right to a higher standard than those of another nation. "Although even the most perfect international solidarity could hardly bring about perfect equality among nations," he said, "still there is an urgent need that this solidarity be achieved, at least in measure enough to change appreciably the present situation. This is far indeed from a just harmony." In other words solidarity among nations demands the abolition of glaring inequalities in living standards.

Yet again what exactly does "equality" mean? Pius XII in his address to members of the International Congress for Social Studies of June 3rd, 1950, made a point all too often overlooked. There is indeed, he argued, an obligation to help the under-developed peoples, but those who help them often assume with absurd naïveté that these people's conception of the good life is exactly the same as that of their helpers—whether those helpers be Russian Communists or American or European capitalists. On the contrary we must help them, said the pope, to improve their own lives. We must not ruthlessly smash their pattern and attempt to impose upon them a crude copy of our own pattern. Pius XII said:

> As to the countries where industrialism begins today to be envisaged, we can only lend the weight of the ecclesiastical authorities to sparing populations, which have lived until now in a patriarchal or feudal régime and above all in diverse groups, the repetition of the grievous omissions of economic liberalism in the last century . . . Even with regard to this new industrialization the question still remains; does i t or does it not contribute to the reintegration and security of a healthy productivity in the national economy? Or alternatively, does it only multiply still further the number of industries always at the mercy of recurring crises? And then, where the investment of capital is guided only by the desire for short-lived advantages and where an empty pride in national prestige determines economic decisions, what care will be taken to consolidate and develop the home market, made productive by reason of the importance of the population and the multiplicity of its needs?

Even this problem of preserving the pattern of native life is not a simple one, for alike in Asia and in South America one of the main causes of poverty is undoubtedly the extortion of the landlord who sucks the wealth out of the peasant and uses his own wealth for "conspicuous waste" rather than for investment. "Every plan or programme," said Pius XII again in his Christmas broadcast of 1942, "must be inspired by the principle that man as subject, guardian and promoter of human values, is more important than mere things, is more important than the practical applications of scientific progress and that, above all, it is imperative to preserve from an unwholesome 'depersonalization,' as it may be described, the essential forms of the social order."

The phrase "social justice" first used, as it seems, by the Jesuit Taparelli d'Azeglio in 1840, made its first appearance in a papal document in *Quadragesimo Anno*. Pius XII in his encyclical on atheistic Communism wrote:

> It is of the very essence of social justice to demand from each individual all that is necessary for the common good. But, just as in the living organism, it is impossible to provide for the good of the whole unless each single part and each individual member is given what it needs for the exercise of its proper functions, so it is impossible to care for the social organism and the good of society as a unit unless each single part and each individual member— that is, each individual man in the dignity of his human personality—is supplied with all that is necessary for the exercise of his social functions.

"The goods created by God for all men," he wrote in *Sertum Laetitiae*, "should in the same way reach all, justice guiding and charity helping." Such quotations show admirably that the Catholic position is a balanced and central position, insisting alike on the rights of the individual and the rights of society. They do not, the critic might object, show us the principle by which we can be assured that we have struck the balance. In the same way Canon Janssens in the first number of *World Justice* tells us that policy should have three essential objects: (1) to enable all people to share in the economic goods of the world, (2) to provide a proper health service for everybody, (3) to provide education for everybody. Admirable, but what precisely is a "due" share, a "proper" health service, a sufficient education?

We must record the undoubted fact that, by and large, the West has exported its material techniques but has not exported its religion to the Orient. We must insist that the Catholic should, wherever possible, cooperate with the non-Catholic in works of economic betterment and note the care with which the popes put forward economic doctrines in language as acceptable as possible to the non-Catholic and the non-Christian. But, when Pius XII adds that in proportion as humanity works for the fulfilment of the natural law "humanity will become steadily more disposed to become the Mystical Body of Christ,"[5] when Cardinal Lercaro writes, "the community is still to be built, and built up from its foundation, can exist and can have the force of a community only to the extent to which it receives its spirit and its breath of life from that unique community which was established from on high and which alone comprises Man and his whole history in Christ and through Christ,"[6] they are not indulging in mere flights of pious rhetoric. Christianity is not merely the religion of God; it is the religion of God who became Man.

Therefore history, the story of Man, has a significance to the Christian which it can never have to the follower of a religion that is purely a religion of the other world. The secularist who pins all his hopes on progress in this world, indeed exaggerates the importance of this world, but, had it not been for the generations of Christians behind him, he would never have thought of progress in this world as possible. Christianity freely recognizes that the great non-Christian religions have many incidental truths to teach. It welcomes their witness to these truths—the witness of Hindu and Buddhist to the immanence of God and of Jew and Mohammedan to his transcendence—claiming that in the Christian revelation alone is the perfect balance achieved. As Pius said to the Indian Catholics on December 31st, 1952, "Make it understood that everything that is true, and everything that is good in other religions, finds a deeper meaning and likewise

5 *Allocution to the Catholic Youth of Italy*. March 19th, 1956.
6 *La Communauté mondiale et l'universalisme chrétienne*, p. 96.

its completion in Christ." Yet the gospel of secular progress—
what Pius XII called in *Fidei Donum* "the fallacious prestige
of technical civilization"—has dealt to non-Christian religions
blows so damaging that it is unlikely that they will ever again
recapture their power over the minds of their followers, but
because of its inherent unreason it can never in itself satisfy
its adherent. Its adherent, whether in Europe or in Asia, can
only find satisfaction when he turns from the partial faith in
secular progress to the full faith of Christian revelation, from
which it derives, forgetful or ignorant as it may be of its
derivation.

All talk about a world united by economic progress must of
course face another criticism. It may be, says the critic, that
the world ought to be united, but most certainly it is disunited.
Side by side with economic developments, which in truth
demand a recognition of unity, have gone political developments by which the world is fragmented into a greater number
than ever before of petty national states, each claiming
absolute sovereignty, each jealous of its neighbour. In particular how can you talk of world unity when the world is
manifestly divided into two gigantic power blocs—Communist
and non-Communist with, between them, a vast uncom-
mitted area for whose allegiance they are in rivalry? This is not
the place to examine the nature of Communism, the development of Communist power politics or the possibilities of
peaceful co-existence, but there are certain propositions which
are relevant to this study and which should be clearly stated.
Communism is clearly incompatible with Christianity. This
has been stated without reservation alike from the papal and
the Marxian side and it is indeed self-evident from the writings
of Marx and Lenin. Therefore no Catholic can be a Communist. It is not so much that the pope has forbidden it as
that the laws of logic forbid a contradiction. But it does not
follow in logic that the Catholic need necessarily be at physical
war with the Communist, refuse to trade with him for mutual
advantage, refuse to have any dealings with him—above all
refuse to love him. Every prophecy of the New Testament bids

the Catholic expect to be a member of a small—probably persecuted—minority and be prepared to have relations with non-Catholic fellow beings. There may (or there may not) have been a time when the Communists were so weak and unstable in power that they could have been arrested and suppressed by something of the nature of police action, and it might (or might not) have been desirable at that time to have taken such action. That we need not now discuss. It is clear that they cannot be thus easily overthrown now—that, whether we like it or not, there is now no alternative to co-existence but co-destruction.

Evil and tyrannical as many of the actions of Communists have been, there is no demand from the Catholic Church, and no sane demand from anywhere in the Western world, for a war for their forcible overthrow. Indeed, such hope as there is for an amelioration of their tyrannical conduct at home clearly depends upon an atmosphere of peace. They are not likely to be more generous towards dissidents so long as they feel themselves threatened from without. But the difficulty of peaceful coexistence comes not from Western unwillingness but from a doubt whether the Communists sincerely believe in its possibility. This is not the place to attempt to unwrap the enigma of Soviet policy. The evidence is abundant that both Marx and Lenin believed a violent physical conflict between the Communist and the non-Communist worlds to be inevitable. Any peaceful coexistence that they would have contemplated would have been merely tactical and ephemeral. Stalin's opinion was probably the same. There is reason to think that, with the development of the new weapons, the present régime in Russia has modified its views. It thinks rightly that a military conflict between East and West would result in the destruction of both and it is anxious to avoid it. But, even if that be so—as it probably is—it would be naïve to imagine that Mr Krushchev and his colleagues—still less, the Chinese leaders—believe in peaceful coexistence in the sense that they believe that our régimes and their régimes can live side by side peacefully together for the rest of time. They have never made any pretence of believing that. They have always been quite frank in their prophecies that the collapse of the non-Communist régimes is inevitable because of their inherent contradictions, and that the whole world, eventually and probably before very long, is destined to have Communist governments. Only they now think that, so long as they are prepared to bide their time, such revolutions can be made without war.

This is not the place for an analysis of Marxian teaching or for speculation how far Marxian prophecies are likely to be found accurate. We are only concerned with judging how far the fact that Communists hold such beliefs must have its effect on Catholic teaching. We can approach the whole problem of the underdeveloped countries in two quite different ways —what might be called the idealistic and the realistic way. It is possible to argue on pure Christian principles that the have's should help the have-not's—that we have a Christian duty to make investments for the development of the under-developed countries. We can fairly point to the large sums of money which through various agencies have been given or lent—mainly by Americans—to such countries since the war. No other period of history can show a record that even begins to compare with it. Yet, naturally enough, the cynic replies by asking how far such generosity has been inspired by true Christian principles and by genuine love for the under-privileged. On the contrary, he will say, these are mere bribes to prevent the Orientals from going over to the Communists and of that the Oriental is well aware and therefore he feels small gratitude for such gifts or loans. It would of course be silly to deny that the motive of such policies has largely been the desire to spoil the market for the Communists—that there is every reason to think that, had there not been a Communist menace, much less would have been done—and that to some extent and on occasion assistance has been given, not at the place or in the form in which it was ideally most needed, but as it might immediately be most convenient for a strategy of resistance to Communism.

The would-be recipients of aid of course also understand all this well enough and equally to some extent and on occasion they have astutely played off the West against the Communists, threatening that their country will go Communist unless it is put high on the list of beneficiaries. In the name of a sturdy nationalism they have demanded that aid be "without strings". It sounds well—and indeed there is some sincerity in the demand—but the fact that it is administered by native officials has again all too often meant that much of the aid stuck on the way and never got through to those for whom it was designed. All these things are true and should be said and understood in order to save us from the folly of over simplifying a very complicated moral issue. But equally we must avoid the counter-folly which thinks that, if a thing is not done perfectly, it is not worth doing at all. Among fallen men no good action is ever done for utterly good reasons or in utterly good ways. Motives are always mixed and execution is imperfect, but that does not say that good actions should not be done. It would doubtless be much better that the Russians should forget their rivalry with us, should remember only the sufferings of the poor, should join with us in an entirely sincere and disinterested campaign for the relief of that poverty. But it would be idle to expect that that will easily happen and foolish to wait for it to happen before we take any action of our own.

CHAPTER V

CATHOLICISM AND THE POPULATION QUESTION

THE SHIFTING BALANCE OF POPULATION

The question of the precise machinery through which investment in the underdeveloped countries can most conveniently
be directed is a technical and not a Catholic question. All that
we can demand of the Catholic, as a Catholic, is that he play
his full part in this work, which is undoubtedly a Catholic
work. But, playing his full part, he can perhaps also, from the
traditions of his faith, put the problem into a better proportion
to the larger problem of the end of man than can the mere
technocrat. In general, as has been argued, the Church does
not lay down detailed economic policies. Yet there is one
problem on which the Church has definite teaching that must
necessarily have its bearing on economic solutions. This is
the question of population. Certainly throughout history one
of the most potent causes of wars has been the shifting balance
of population between one nation and another. The inhabitants
of the nations that have flattered themselves that they are
the leaders of civilization have from Roman times onwards
always had the ambition to impose peace on the world, and
their conception of peace has been broadly the preservation of
a status quo which leaves them still in their predominant
position. Those who threatened such an arrangement were
denounced as barbarians from outside the civilized world. Yet
by what appeared to be an almost inevitable law the birth-rate

in the countries of the higher standard of living fell. That among their more barbarous neighbours remained high, until eventually the more fecund barbarians broke in and seized the possessions of those who had failed in the task of replenishing their stock. No single formula can sum up the whole complex story of human history, but the shifting balance of populations probably comes nearer to explaining the causes of war than any other. No prophecy of perpetual peace that does not make allowance for it can hope to succeed.

Now this is clearly of importance for our study because it deals with a matter on which the Church has definite teaching. In economic affairs in general, as has been argued, the difference between the Catholic and the non-Catholic is not sundering. The pope tells the Catholic what questions to ask but the questions are to a large extent the same questions that any man of good will would ask. Catholic and non-Catholic alike can devote themselves to the common good and may easily find a large measure of identity of opinion as to how that common good can best be served. Many a man who is quite unable to accept the Christian faith may yet find himself in agreement with much that the pope teaches, and anyone who prefers his selfish ends to the common good suffers the reproaches of his conscience, whether he be a Christian or not.

BIRTH CONTROL

But, when we come to birth control, we come to quite a different situation. There we have to recognize that there are many people—many even who sincerely call themselves Christians—who most honestly do not think that it is invariably wrong to use contraceptives. Not only do they use them but their conscience does not reproach them for using them. The Catholic Church is today, I fancy, the only body which as a body condemns the use of contraceptives in any circumstances.

This is not the place either to define in detail—still less to defend—the Church's teaching on contraceptives. But in a study of the Church's economic teaching it is necessary to consider the economic consequences of her teaching about birth control. Contraceptives are of course freely used by those who live an entirely incontinent life, but such a life is plainly contrary to any conception of Christianity, nor is it difficult to show that it is also contrary to any conception of good citizenship. Yet it is not only the incontinent who use contraceptives. If we would controvert a case, it is necessary to controvert it at its strongest, not at its weakest. Our concern is not with the wholly incontinent but with those conscientious persons who argue on moral and, as they would say, sometimes on Christian grounds, that there are occasions when contraceptives should be used.

Contraceptives are defended, roughly, for three reasons—the medical, the aesthetic and the economic. On the medical ground it is argued that it is indeed desirable that parents should have a reasonable family but that that family should be spaced out. There are often occasions when, for medical or economic reasons, it is not immediately desirable or possible to have another child. Sometimes for medical reasons it is not possible to have another child at all. Even the Catholic Church, runs the argument, does not under these circumstances command complete abstinence. It permits the use of the notoriously unsafe "safe" period. If you are allowed to control births, what advantage can there be in controlling them in an unreliable rather than in the more reliable ways that are available?

Or again with the aesthetic argument. There are those who say, "I do not know whether the world could sustain a larger population or not, but why should it? It would patently be a much pleasanter place if there were fewer people in it." The commuter caught in a six o'clock rush on a London underground or a New York subway or the inhabitant of some old-world village who finds a new rash of council houses springing up to spoil his view may be tempted to sympathize with this feeling. Recently I was in Kenya and talking to a white hunter who was complaining that owing to the encroachments of an increasing human population the wild animals in Eastern Africa would be virtually extinct in a dozen years. One can have understanding of all these points of view. Indeed the Catholic has probably a stronger natural bias in favour of the preservation of traditional patterns of life than has the non-Catholic, and it certainly appears at first sight, at any rate, that the preservation of these patterns would be much easier if population was stable. Still, these arguments are not strictly speaking economic arguments and it would be beyond our purpose to develop here the traditional Catholic answers to them. Our concern is with the economic argument.

It is a serious argument and deserves to be fairly stated and seriously considered. It is important to do so because its proponents—and not only its popular proponents, but even those who can speak with the authority of scientists or thinkers of the standing of Professor Toynbee—often put it in an exaggerated form. There are two propositions which it is common to hear advanced. One is that the world's population is increasing so rapidly that, unless some means to check it are soon discovered, an explosion in the near future is inevitable. The other is that since England is one of the most thickly populated countries in the world and since England's population is still increasing, it is desirable to reduce the population in this country. Both of these propositions, commonly advanced as they are, are certainly fallacious.

INCREASE OF POPULATION MATCHED BY INCREASED FOOD PRODUCTION

Of course the world's population is rapidly increasing, but it is certainly not increasing as rapidly as the world's production of food. We are often told that the gap between the standards of the "have" and the "have-not" countries is widening. The gap may be widening—it is difficult to know exactly how it should be measured when the goods consumed are so very different—but, if so, that is only because the standards in the "have" countries are increasing with such very great rapidity. There is no reason at all to say that the standards of Oriental countries are falling absolutely with the increase in their population. On the contrary the food production in the world has been increasing since 1948 by 2·7% per annum—almost twice as fast as the population.

It is quite true that that increase has been most spectacular in the "have" countries which have already more than a sufficiency of food and there is indeed an urgent problem how to distribute the surplus of the "have's"[1] so that it passes into the mouths of the "have-nots" instead of being stored uselessly in bins, but, real as that problem is, nevertheless in the Far East over the last ten years food production has increased by 3% per annum and population by 1·4%. In India in 1949–50 the intake of food was 1,620 calories per day per person, in 1953–54 1,900 and in 1959 it was estimated that it had risen to 2,000. It is difficult to get reliable statistics of what is happening in China, but there is no doubt that, in spite of the failure of the Chinese Five Year Plan to reach its targets, it yet succeeded in substantially increasing production. Industrial production in the Far East has increased even more rapidly than agricultural production. During the last ten years it has almost tripled, rising from 57 to 156 with 1953 as the base year, while that of the world at large only rose from 68 to 132. Of course there is appalling poverty in the underdeveloped countries of the world and no policy is going to remove that poverty in a sudden moment. But there is no reason to think that poverty is in general the consequence of overpopulation—rather the reverse. Famine in the East is no new thing. What is new is that anyone should think of remedying it. Throughout all the past history of the East it has been taken for granted. It has been taken for granted because communications were so bad that those who were not on the scene of the famine did not hear about it nor was it possible for them to bring relief even had they wanted to. The protection against famine is an efficient system of communications, and an efficient system of communications is only economical in a reasonably thickly populated country. There has of course been what Mr Nehru has called "a revolution in expectations". People in the East, as elsewhere,

[1] Zimmerman, *Overpopulation*, pp. 3, 4.

want more than their ancestors wanted and will no longer be content, as their ancestors were content, with a standard of living fantastically lower than that of the white man. It would be hypocritical for a white man to blame them for this, and I say no word in criticism of schemes for raising the standard and variety of life of such people. Such schemes should be supported and it may very well be that there would be an explosion if we of the West refused to support them. But the cause of the explosion would not be starvation but envy.

The population of the world, it is estimated, was 1,810 million in 1920, 2,031 million in 1930, 2,246 million in 1940, 2,476 million in 1950 and 2,737 million in 1956.[2] There are those who say that, increase food production as we may, the amount of land in the world is limited and, if population increases indefinitely, a breaking point is bound to be reached eventually. Thus Malthus argued a hundred and fifty years ago, and, although the possibilities of expansion have proved to be much greater than Malthus ever envisaged, the proposition is certainly true as an abstract proposition, but Professor Colin Clark is certainly also correct in asserting that the limits of population which the world is capable of supporting are enormously greater than is commonly supposed. Probably half of the world's area is cultivable and one tenth is cultivated. It is true that the new land brought into cultivation would be likely to be less fertile than the land at present cultivated, but it is also true that by irrigation, by measures against erosion, by sensible use of fertilizers and other methods of scientific agriculture, vast increases in the yield of land at present cultivated are possible.

If we brought into cultivation all cultivable land, Professor Clark has calculated, the world would be capable of supporting a population of 28 billion—ten times its present figure—at Dutch standards, or of 90 billion if we chose to go over to a predominantly cereal diet.[3] Nor is there any danger of an

[2] Zimmerman, *op. cit.*, p. 2.
[3] Colin Clark, "The World Can Feed Its People." *World Justice*, Vol. 1, p. 49.

exhaustion of fuel. Even if supplies of petroleum should prove inadequate—which is improbable—it would be possible to produce sufficient motor fuel from shale, from coal or from compressed hydrogen. The estimated number of years' supply of minerals for a world population of 28 billion consuming at the same rate per head as the population of the United States in 1957 is [4]

Aluminium	$3 \cdot 1 \times 10^8$	Lead	$1 \cdot 2 \times 10^5$
Iron	5×10^6	Zinc	3×10^5
Copper	$5 \cdot 5 \times 10^5$	Tin	1×10^5

So it is evident that the world has a considerable time before it is likely to die of starvation and there is little reason to doubt that long before that happens new forms of nuclear-created wealth will be available. Nor is there a danger of a shortage of capital. The economically advanced nations set aside about 10% of their annual incomes in savings. Even allowing for a population-increase at home of 2% per annum, they only require about 5% to maintain their domestic standards. They have therefore 5% to spare for the under-developed countries.

The industrial development of the non-white countries of the world has as yet scarcely begun. As we can see from the example of Russia, when a country is industrialized, unless indeed it is financed from outside itself, it has doubtless to go through a period of hardship and shortage of consumer goods but then finds itself after a period capable of a quite fantastic-ally increased productivity. There is no reason at all to think that this is not the future in store for the Asian and African countries. Their industrialization and increased productivity will create grave problems both for them and for us, but a danger of world starvation is not one of them. The real problem is not whether they can increase their production but whether they can increase it without adopting totalitarian forms of government.

Now it is certainly true that there are at present the widest

[4] Colin Clark, *art. cit.*, p. 52.

differences in efficiency between one nation and another. In the far East Java, in spite on the whole of greater natural advantages, has a rice yield per acre only a third of that of Japan. India, according to Jerome Ziliak,[5] is producing at only about a tenth of her capacity. It is reasonable to hope that backward nations will learn lessons from more progressive nations and that there will be a general increase of efficiency, as indeed there has already been on so enormous a scale. The sane question to ask is not, How shall we restrict population? but rather, How shall we eliminate those unnecessary wasteful conflicts, on which so much energy and so many resources are now dissipated, so that the world may produce the goods which it is capable of producing and which will be amply sufficient to sustain its population in any foreseeable future? The tensions of the world are not so much the consequence as the cause of its poverty. For modern weapons not only threaten us with the ultimate calamity of annihilating war but, even during the period of uneasy peace, the cost of them is for ever enormously increasing.

FALLACIOUS ARGUMENTS FOR RESTRICTION OF POPULATION

Similarly the notion that a restriction of population is desirable in England, or the United States, or any Western European country, arises from a mere misunderstanding of the statistics. It is easy, balancing the figures of births for a current year against the figures of deaths, to say, should the births exceed the deaths, that population is increasing and to deduce from that that it will continue to increase, unless there is some drastic change in people's habits. The conclusion seems obvious but it is fallacious. The number of births depends not on one factor but on two—on the number of children born per woman and the number of women of childbearing age. If there has been a period of a very high birthrate, when the average husband and wife produced substantially more than the "two plus" number of children that

5 Quoted by Zimmerman, *op. cit.*, pp. 10, 11.

are necessary for the population to replace itself, then it is obvious that the total population, when those children grow up, will be substantially larger. But supposing that those children break with their parents' habits and produce in their time much smaller families, then for a generation the total population may still continue to increase because, though the average family is smaller, there are a larger number of families. But, if the birth rate is no longer up to the figure of "two plus" which is necessary for replacement, then the total population will indeed go on increasing so long as there are still people alive who were born in the past period of larger families, but, when those people die off, the increase will cease and the total population will begin to decline.

Birth-rates oscillate a good deal. There have been periods —as, for instance, the years immediately after the war—when the birth-rate in Western countries rose considerably, only later to fall again. No one can therefore prophesy with certainty what will be the birth-rate of future years, but there is at least far greater danger that it will be found that we are now living through that intermediate period when the birth-rate is no longer sufficient to reproduce the population but where the decline has not yet shown itself in a positively declining total population than it is that our problem in the future will be a problem of overpopulation.

From time to time we read estimates from the pens of popularizing journalists of world population or world food supplies at some distant future date. Such estimates are worthless. Even if we may assume some small steady decline in death rates, no one can prophesy what will be the future fluctuations of birth-rates. Still less can anyone prophesy world food production at any distant future date. Nuclear power may by then have destroyed the human race, or, if harnessed to peaceful purposes, it may have made possible unimaginable increases in the world's production. All that we can say is that there is of course a theoretical possibility that the world's population will exceed its resources but that any suggestion that we are in sight of that happening is false.

There is a good deal of evidence that with higher standards of living birth-rates almost inevitably fall. Anyone, therefore, who prophesies that, as they become industrialized, the birth-rates of the Russians, of the Southern Europeans and in their turn of the Indians or of the Chinese will fall, is very likely to be proved a true prophet. If so and as the rates fall below the reproduction rate, then indeed the populations of these countries will in the end begin to fall. But, as has been shown by the previous argument, that fall will not begin to show itself in a total reduction of numbers for some time, whereas the fall in the Western populations, since Western populations have already had a falling birth-rate for nearly a century, will begin to show itself much sooner. Already the white proportion of the world's population is steadily declining. Therefore the advocates of birth control, while recommending it to the West, also recommend it, and with much greater enthusiasm, to the Orientals. They are indeed logical to do so. Wars throughout history have been caused not so much by a growing population over the world or by a falling population over the world as by a difference of population-behaviour between one country and another—a falling population in one country and a growing population in another. If there were a falling population all over the world, then we should all have a falling standard of living, since, until population is so thick that we cannot find raw materials with which the producer can produce— which is far from happening yet—the more producers that there are, the more can each producer produce per head, through the advantages of mass production, and the more therefore each consumer can receive. Yet we might well have a political stability of a sort since no nation would have any especial motive to expand at its neighbour's expense. But that is not in the least the situation with which we are likely to be confronted. The Western propagandist for birth control may well say to the Indian and the Chinese, "Would it not be a good plan that you should restrict your populations and thus help us to achieve stability?" But it is far from certain that the Indian and the Chinese will agree. It is more likely that they will say, "When you speak of stability, what you mean is a perpetuation of a division of the world's wealth highly to your own advantage. If you do not wish to take the trouble to reproduce yourselves, why should we accept that division? We prefer to increase our numbers and to take advantage of the increase in order to push you out of territories that you have no right to occupy." *Birth Control—A Plot To Kill Negroes*, runs a notice on a wall at Kingston, Jamaica.

If the Orientals should decide for themselves to restrict their births, as indeed the Japanese are now restricting them—even though through what is to most people the repugnant habit of legalizing abortion—that is something that we can do little about, but the suggestion has been put forward in certain Western circles that the adoption of policies of birth control should be imposed on Oriental countries as a condition of economic aid. The Draper Committee made such a recommendation to the American President in July, 1959. This is surely a suggestion of strange psychological ineptitude. If, as we are often told, the Oriental nations object to "strings" of a political or military nature being attached to their aid, how much more are they likely to object to a condition which interferes with the most intimate conduct of their private life? The Oriental to a large extent reckons happiness by the number of his or her children. It may be that changing circumstances will make him in the course of time less philoprogenitive. To attempt crudely to bribe him into these new attitudes would invite explosion.

Thus, specious as they superficially appear, the large generalized demands for world birth-control are found on examination to be of very little force. I do not, as I say, by asserting this deny that there are particular cases of great difficulty. Sincere and compassionate people, as I have admitted, plead that it is the lesser evil to use contraceptives, where for medical reasons a child is at the moment not desirable. It is not an economic question nor is it within our terms of reference to consider why the Church permits the safe period and condemns contraceptives, or to enter into the border-line debates. On the economic plane it can cogently be argued that perhaps it has been shown that over all it is desirable that the world should have a larger population— that, if only all the world were organized as efficiently as Holland, there would be no difficulty in supporting such a population. But all the world is not organized as efficiently as Holland nor is it likely to be. If mere generalizations cannot be legitimately invoked to support policies of birth control, equally mere generalizations cannot be invoked to condemn them. The world may not in general be overpopulated but particular places obviously are overpopulated. What comfort is it to an Indian peasant, whose baby is likely to starve, to be told that the bins of Canada are bursting and that India herself is capable of producing ten times as much food as she is producing? What can she do about it? What can the dweller in a Glasgow slum do to break down restrictive practices and trade barriers but for which, she is told, there would be an abundance for all? She wants to know what she may do here and now in a world in which doubtless many foolish policies are pursued but over whose policies she has no control. What use is it to tell the people of Barbados to be fruitful and multiply and that the world is not overcrowded? Barbados is overcrowded, and they are in Barbados.

Pius XII, for instance, said in his Christmas Broadcast for 1952:

> We are thinking of the consequences of poverty and still more of the consequences of utter want and misery. For some families there is a dying daily, a dying hourly, a dying multiplied, especially for parents, by the number of dear ones they behold suffering and wasting away. Meanwhile sickness is all the more serious because not properly treated; it strikes the little ones in particular, because preventive measures are lacking. Then there is the weakening and consequent physical deterioration of whole generations. Whole masses of the population are brought up as enemies of law and order, so many poor girls gone astray, driven down into the bottom of the abyss, because they believed that that was the only way out of their shameful poverty.

IMMIGRATION AND EMIGRATION

Now it does obviously follow, as we can see from Pius XII's words, that it is no use resting a case on world economic conditions alone unless there is substantial world freedom of movement so that the individual, unable to find an opening at home, can try his luck elsewhere. Before the nineteenth century populations, owing to the gigantic infant mortality, altered comparatively slowly. Owing to the poverty of communications both trade and migration, for all the controversy about them, were of almost negligible dimensions in comparison with those of later times. With the nineteenth century and the industrial revolution the whole nature of the problem changed. There was a new sort of economy which for its success required a degree of freedom hitherto alike unknown and unnecessary. By and large the nineteenth century accepted that requirement. Government restrictions on trade were small compared with those to which we have become accustomed in our own times, and Britain, the leading trading nation, followed from the middle of the century a policy of complete free trade.

What between industrial and medical progress there was a gigantic increase in the numbers of people of European birth in that century. The European countries with their developing economies were able to absorb within their own territories a substantial proportion of that increase, but it would not have been possible for them to absorb it all without explosions. Explosions were avoided because there was free migration, and those Europeans who could not obtain jobs at home were able without restriction to make their homes in the new countries overseas—in North or South America or in Australia. Since the First World War the new countries have severely restricted migration, though a happy panic has caused Australia in recent years to adopt a more liberal policy. That restriction of migration has certainly been one of the main causes of the world's troubles. The Church has no definite teaching on migration or the freedom of trade similar to her teaching on birth control. She does not tell statesmen that it is a mortal sin to restrict immigration for reasons of health or if there should be at the moment a large domestic unemployment. The statesman is entitled to pay regard to the cultural and racial traditions of his country and to regulate immigration at such a pace that it does not destroy the native way of life and create social discord. There is no obligation to receive immigrants whom it is not possible to absorb. The pace of immigration may sometimes have to be regulated, if a way of life is to be preserved. Nevertheless, even though the Church makes no dogmatic rulings and leaves it to statesmen to shape the details of their own policy, balancing one good against another, yet the general bias of the Church must necessarily be in favour of as much freedom of migration and freedom of trade as possible. "It is not without significance," said Pius XII in his address to members of the Congress of Chambers of Commerce on April 27th, 1950, "that in mythology Mercury has been endowed with wings. Must it not seem as a symbol of free movement which a trader needs both within and without the frontiers of his own country?" Again, in his broadcast of June 1st, 1941, Pius XII said:

It is on occasion inevitable that some families should emigrate to seek a new homeland. . . . We should like to see a better distribution of mankind over the surface of the earth which God has created and provided for everyone's use. If the two sides (those allowing emigration from their shores and those welcoming the newcomers) continue to act with mutual consideration and faithfully remove every impediment to a birth of a genuine trust between the country of emigration and the country of immigration, everyone will benefit from such a change of place and people.

In his radio message given on the anniversary of *Rerum Novarum* Pius XII said yet again:

All men, considered as living creatures endowed with reason, derive from nature the right to make use of the fruits of the earth, though the detailed regulation of this right may be left to the human will and to the legal system of the State. An individual right of this kind is not to be abrogated in any way, not even by other unquestionable and recognized rights to goods. No doubt the natural order, since it proceeds from God, calls for private property and the free traffic in goods by exchange and gifts, as also for the control by the authority of the State of both these institutions. Nevertheless, all these things remain subordinate to the natural purpose of material goods.

The Church does not demand that Catholics obstinately deny the reality of racial differences or shut their eyes to the fact that intermarriage presents problems which must be treated on their merits rather than swept away in broad generalization. Yet Christ died for all men and for all women. All souls are of value in God's sight and the tendency of Catholicism must necessarily be to demand that racial differences be emphasized as little as possible. It is certainly important in the modern world that this influence of the Church in favour of freedom should be as strong as possible. The restrictions on immigration into the countries of the new world after the First World War were certainly one of the main causes of the tension which eventually exploded into the Second World War. The white races today, rightly or wrongly, have determined to acquire for themselves a higher standard of living. They proclaim that standard as the test and object of their policies. Now that higher standard of living can only be acquired if they are prepared to trade and to buy raw materials from every quarter of the globe. Such trade can only be carried on if they are willing to mix with people of other races much more freely than they have done in the past, and it goes without saying that you cannot mix in business unless you are prepared to mix socially and to tolerate at any rate the occasional mixed marriage. Racial tolerance and racial intermixture in the modern world are therefore necessary alike on economic and on Christian grounds.

SELECT BIBLIOGRAPHY

In this series: LECLERQ, Jacques: *Christianity and Money.*

BRODRICK, James, S. J.: *The Economic Morals of the Jesuits,* London and New York, Oxford Univ. Press, 1934.

BRUEHL, Charles D.: *The Pope's Plan for Social Reconstruction,* New York, Devin Adair, 1949.

CLARK, Colin: *The Conditions of Economic Progress,* London, Macmillan, and New York, St Martin's Press, 3rd edn, 1957.

CRONIN, John S.: *Catholic Social Principles,* Milwaukee, Bruce, 1955.

FREMANTLE, Anne (Editor): *The Papal Encyclicals in their Historical Context,* New York, New American Library of World Literature, 1956.

GILL, Eric: *Christianity and the Machine Age,* London, Sheldon Press, 1940.

HALES, E. E. Y.: *The Catholic Church in the Modern World,* London, Eyre and Spottiswoode, 1958.

HOLLIS, Christopher: *The Breakdown of Money,* London and New York, Sheed and Ward, 1937.

HUGHES, Philip: *The Popes' New Order: A Systematic Study of the Social Encyclicals and Addresses from Leo XIII to Pius XII,* London, Burns Oates, 1943.

KEYNES, J. M.: *Essays in Persuasion,* London, Macmillan, 1931; *A Treatise on Money,* two volumes, London, Macmillan, and New York, Harcourt, 1930; *The General Theory of Employment, Investment and Money,* London, Macmillan, and New York, Harcourt, 1939.

ORR, Boyd J.: *The White Man's Dilemma,* London, Allen and Unwin, 1958.

SOMERVILLE, H.: *Studies on the Catholic Social Movement*, London, Burns Oates, 1933.

WILLIAMS, M. J.: *Catholic Social Thought*, New York, Ronald Press, 1954.

ZIMMERMAN, A. E.: *Overpopulation*, Washington, Catholic Univ. Press, 1958.